OPEN ROAD

I lie still looking up. The gauzy film above my head shrouds the trees and everything appears in grays and blacks. It is this view that I have longed for all my life. I have taken to the road to explore the country and most importantly who I am.

PROLOGUE

I grew up reading cowboy books, books on horses and the open sky, but I lived the city life with streetlights and car horns. I wanted something more than this sterile world. I wanted to be able to jump on my horse and ride amongst the pines, to see the sunset over the hills and smell the good earth. I wanted to play with my dog in the mud and spend hours in the woods climbing and searching for creepy crawly things to scare my sister. My childhood memories are not made up of these natural scenes, they are of one caught in the forests of tall straight trees with branches of wire and the intense smell of macadam from the heat of the long day. My horse that I longed for was made of metal and rubber. It carried me across the open parking lots and graveyards taking me home to our cement covered yard. As I biked I would look up and see the street lights outlined by the orange night sky and the gray haze of the moon peaking around the houses. I longed for open sky and stars, not the grey horizon caused by so many lights and pollution. Maybe I would grow up and live, where I could look out upon the trees and not see the glow of one single street light.

CHAPTER ONE
PREMONITION

I have left behind the street lights, the sirens and the pavement. I have come so far but not far enough. I look up, and in that moment catch a glimpse of a shooting star. The milky way shines down upon me and I can listen to the movement of the leaves in the still night air. I want to be able to share my life with someone but I need to know what makes me happy, to be able to make someone else happy. I think this will be the start of the end of one chapter in my life and the beginning of the beginning of the rest of my life.

We were ready. I packed the car three times and tried all sorts of configurations to get everything in. I was actually trying to be organized. I settled on the smallest amount of stuff in the car. I put everything in. As I was doing this Raven and Bristol patiently sat at the gate and watched me. Worry stretched across their features. They kept looking at me making sure that they were going.

"Yes, you are going.... see all the leashes and dog stuff here". I pointed to the dog stuff hanging off the stall divider I was going to use as a barrier for the dogs. Raven and Bristol just peered into the car. When I loaded up the double dog beds, Raven jumped in and sighed.

"Well, guess that is your spot, Ray" I turned to see Bristol sitting there looking at me expectantly... "Yes, you can get in." He leaped into the car and turned around and rested his head on the divider. I smiled and continued to pack the rest of the stuff into the roof "coffin" and was happy to see that the "kids" were pleased with this arrangement.

"I still can't believe I am actually going." I say to myself. At that moment the phone rings, it was my sister so I picked it up. "Hey Tiny what's up... I'm packing and need both hands."

"Just wanted to see if you need anything?"

"Nope, still trying to figure out the packing thing."

"How are the dogs taking it?" She says.

"Well, Raven has put herself in the car and Bristol was a quick second. They are making sure I don't leave without them."

She laughs "Ok talk to you later."

"Bye." I continue to put the stuff in but it is getting dark so I make my last preparations and call the dogs and head in. I get ready for the night and look around longingly. I love my home and the forests that surround it. I will miss this place.

That night I lay my head on the pillow and wonder how it will be sleeping in the tent. I have only camped a few times in my life and that was always with a group of people or with another person. A sigh escapes my lips as I slowly realize what I am about to embark on. My eyes close on the fan that is circling lazily above my head and I wonder what I will dream about on the eve of my trip.

I wake up to an overcast day. Everything is packed except the warm bodies, so I walk the dogs along the forest loop one last time and say goodbye to the trees and earth that I walk upon. I touch the trees as I walk amongst them. "I will be back, Mother, I will miss you." I can't stop looking around to make sure that I will remember what it looks like, to be surrounded in green and brown. What will I take with me and what will I bring back? I feel the excitement as I crest the hill and see my house nestled in the trees. I will be back.

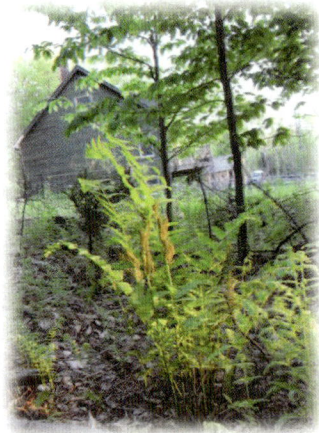

I take one last look at the place as I lock up and head to the jeep. The dogs enthusiastically jump in and I turn the jeep around. It is so silent. The herd of goats are at different farms.

Nina and Stitch were trailered to a friends house last week, so as I pull away from the empty fields I say good-bye to just emptiness. I creep down the driveway unable to believe that I am really on my way. A smile crosses my face as I approach the curve in the drive way and there sits Harold. He sits in the driveway and just looks at me. He cocks his head this way and that and just stares. He is in no rush to move. I take out my phone and take his picture.... it's like he wants to say, "Don't be too long..." I finish taking the picture and beep the horn... The little booger remains there until I rev the engine. He takes one more look at me and waddles off. "Dumb bird," I say, but I smile and head down the driveway. I get to the Y in the road and head for Tiny's house. I don't even get to beep, there she is walking down the stairs. For once in her life she is actually on time. I get out of the car and let the dogs out for one last pee before we head to Angie's. She gives me a big hug and a smile. "You be careful and call me every time you can, to make sure that I know that you are safe."

"Yes, Mom"... I say sarcastically.

"Do you have everything?" She asks. "Yeah, I think so. "K, got to go and get Angie.... See ya." I get back in the car and I head to Angie's to pick her and Vance up. I am headed North East to head West.... hmm that doesn't sound right.   But I am going to start this trip with the one person who I think gets why I am doing it. It feels right.

   I get to Angie's and the dogs pour out and head to see Vance Guy. Angie is ready and we start to pack up.

"Did you bring the kitchen sink too?" I ask her. "You do know that you have to fly back, and there isn't as much room in the plane as there is in the car," I say mockingly to tease her.

"It's Vance's stuff." she says.

"Uh huh" I respond with a smile. After organizing the stuff and pushing the dog beds around we finally get it so that there is some room for the dogs and the luggage, not much room, but, it will do for a couple of hours. Raven and Bristol get up in the jeep and we load up Vance and off we go. Bristol was supposed to be

in the way back but he doesn't like being so far away from Vance so he crawls over all her stuff and leans his head on the child seat with Vance's hand on his head.

"Uh Oh! I hope there isn't anything breakable in those bags." I say to Angie.

"No, it will be ok."

As we pull away from Morrisville, Angie asks, "So you have everything?"

"Yeah... I think so."

"You have the dog licenses."

" Yup."

"The car insurance stuff."

"Yup."

" Your passport?"

"Oh, Shit."

I reach for the phone and call Tiny "Hey can you do me a big favor? I forgot my passport. Can you find it? I think it is in the hutch drawer." I listen as she says ok. "Call me when you get to the house and look for it. Ok?" I reach for the phone when she returns the call. "OK, can't find it in the hutch. I have looked in all the drawers in the kitchen too.... where else would it be?"

"Hell if I know.... um look in the drawers upstairs in my computer desk." I wait as she heads up the stairs. I can hear her feet on the bare boards and I hope that she can find it.

"No? Ok what about looking on the dresser upstairs."

"This is stupid that you left without it."

"I know this is stupid but I really need it if I am going to go through Canada. I guess you could look for it and then send it to Sherri so that I can pick it up when I get there. Where are you now?"

"Upstairs still looking through your computer desk. I am going to look through your night stand.... ok?"

"Yeah, whatever you think." I wait and drive slowly down route 100 hoping that she can find it.

"Yippee... I found it."

"Can you bring it to Waterbury so that I can have it?" I ask with a little bit of a pretty please, sound to my voice.

"Sure, will see you there in 20 min."

So Angie and I head to Waterbury to fill up the car and wait for Tiny. The best laid plans are always full of holes. ☺ We meet at the gas station and she says bye once more. So we head to New York with Vance talking to Bristol and Bristol smiling away.

We get to Angie's mom's house and unload Vance and all the kids' stuff and I repack her stuff so the dogs have a little more room. The back seat can come down now because we don't need the child seat, so they just have some luggage to contend with and they can sleep on that. I head back in with the dogs and we have lunch with her Mom and get ready to leave New England. The first leg of my trip. Headed to the good ole south.

Angie gives Vance a real big hug and then we are on our way. Angie and I are headed to Carlisle Pennsylvania to stay for the night and the next day. Why are we staying for two days in Carlisle? V...e...r...y, good question.

Two months previous:

I walk into the lunch room to see Angie eating her lunch surrounded by other teachers eating and talking over their lunches. She gives me this smile and says, "So I had this premonition last night, well it was sort of a nightmare."

"Yes," I draw out in a guarded sort of way.

"Well, I dreamed that we got into a car accident... and I did see the dogs walking away from it." She trails off.

"What! You say the dogs were walking away but what about us?"

"Well it **is** the same day that I was in that other car accident and hurt my leg. So lots of bad things." And she looks at me sheepishly. Like I'm not going to take that seriously. Ha! Me oh no, not me. I am so dang superstitious that I even think I forced my rottie name Osirus to have a shorter life, because I named him Osirus after the Egyptian god of the dead. What was she thinking?

"We can stay at the hotel if you want." I say this with a bit of a bad premonition too. I am sure her idea of a hotel and mine are completely different. She gives me this look, and yup, it is going to be her idea of a hotel. I look up from my lunch and smile.

"Okay so you find the nice hotel and I will stay there with you, but not too expensive... and don't forget we have the dogs. And they are over 80 lbs." I say with a grin.

"Yeah ok, I will look on the internet. How far are we going to go that first day?"

"I don't know, let's look at that later. Ok?"

"Yeah." She says and she knows that I will go along with her kind of hotel. Jeesh am I a pushover.

So we figured out that Carlisle was about 8-9 hours of

driving and that was good because we would be spending an entire day sitting by the pool or in the hotel room chilling out. So that is why we are headed to Carlisle Pennsylvania for two days not one.

Carlisle Pennsylvania:

We get there at night and she goes in to check in. I wait for her in the car with the dogs. "Got the keys and we got the business suite."
"We have the what?" I say. With a smile, she says. "You'll see."
I open the door to a front room and then a big bedroom with a king size bed. "Not bad I say... How much was this?"
" Only a $100 a night."
" A hundred dollars for ONE night? I knew I shouldn't have asked." She just smiles and hands me the other key card. Oh, well, it is my vacation and I will be sleeping most of the time in the tent and in the car so what the hell. As it turned out it was a great hotel with a nice pool, too. Little did we know it was a dry county and Angie wasn't going to have the margarita next to the pool that she wanted, but it still was a nice place.

It was the first sun we had both seen in a long time so the next day we just hung out at the pool and soaked it up. Well she did. I just visited her for 15 min and in that short amount of time I got a nice tan line that would stick with me for the entire trip. Of course I knew this because it was the only time I used my bathing suit, and are there pockets in a bathing suit? NO. I put my key card in my strap and there it remained for the entire trip. Yup, nice tan lines of my bathing suit and a little funky square on my chest to prove it. Oh we laughed at that one.

CHAPTER 2
SOUTH CAROLINA:

Closed doors

The darkness that surrounded me was complete. I didn't feel the warmth of my own body. I could only hear my breathing and the pounding of my heart. How did I get here? What was to become of me? I slowly reached out to feel the heavy air that enveloped me in its arms. Can I escape? Can I take another breath? I must find the strength inside me. I must take the chance to become what I have longed for…. but what is that exactly? I hope to answer these and the other questions that plague me on this trip. I need to find my Self.

The smell of the heat coming off the pavement brought me back to Georgia, the time of youthful play and damaging decisions.

I walked around the development. Seems like the entire south is one development after another and then a golf course or shopping mall stuck in there randomly. The dogs and I walked along the sidewalks with the fences rising tall along the edge. Not many folks up this early. The sounds of the water sprinklers and the dogs' feet were what filled my ears. The heat of the day was not heavy upon us yet so we could go a while. The live oaks, the beautiful azaleas lined many of the gardens that we walked by. It was like they brought these houses from my old neighborhood in Georgia and just planted them down here. The yards with newly planted silver maples and sod indicating a family from the north, not yet understanding that yes, those trees would grow here but not well. Sod? That would be taken over soon as they figured out that it couldn't compete with the native saw grass. They would find out as I did.

The houses were all dark as we continued down the hill. Curtains drawn against the morning sun, windows shut against the constant humidity. Is this how I lived for so long? Stuck in a house, isolating our selves from each other? Where are the open porches to share an evening with the neighbors? I look around and I do see porches but they are all on the back of the houses. You can't call out to a neighbor as they walk by from there. You can't wave as they drive by. How did it come to this, where we all have our own islands lost in the open sea? Closed doors, closed windows on houses and cars and community.

All of this comes to me as I wander alone through the neighborhood with the dogs. Their panting is now accelerated and I take a last turn and we head back towards the island we are staying on. We arrived late at night after driving for 10 hours or more. I can't seem to remember much. We did do the Skyline drive but it looked so much like Vermont that we left it after an hour and headed to the highway to shoot south. I have been staying with Kathy, Angie's friend, for two days and it was time that I left. It was nice to stay in a wonderful house, and go out to real nice food but I wanted to get on the road. I wanted to start the journey that I had been planning to take for so long. I didn't want to stay here because it reminded me too much of all the pain that I had caused because of selfishness and desire. I needed to leave the south behind me is so many ways.

The reconnection with Dusty was great but he hadn't called me since his dad had died and I was feeling like he didn't want to reconnect. The heat of the south was suffocating me in so many ways. Literally and figuratively. I had to leave.

"Ok we need to take a picture of all of us. Let's do it outside on the porch." I suggested. We shuffle out to the porch and I set up the camera. I look through the view finder and I can't see a thing but white. "The camera needs to get used to the heat and humidity out here. It will be a minute. Let's set up the dogs first and then the camera should be acclimated to this wretched weather." After a moment, "Ok here we go." I hit the timer and run to the porch. "Say cheese." and a chorus of voices ring into the morning and our little island inhabitants are smiling at the camera.

I load the dogs up into the car and we are off to hit the road for Tennessee. It is only a day's drive but it will be the first leg that I will be driving alone. Well, I am not alone. The dogs are watching the traffic with me as we head out of town. "Here we go kids. Are you ready?" They perk up their ears and then figure out that we are just staying in the car and mom is talking out loud. Raven sighs as she puts her head back down on the bed and Bristol smiles at me as his head hangs over the divider. He loves the fact that he can touch mommy. NO metal gate divider behind the front seat.

I leave South Carolina and head north and west. It was my first true WEST direction. It was refreshing to be alone. It was great with Angie but now I could drive 62 without dirty looks. No, really, it was exhilarating to know that this was the first leg of my journey. I was off to see Devlin, a friend who I had lost touch with for 8 years and now have reconnected with. It was time. I felt like I was on the road and it was my time. I was going along the rolling hills and watching the folks pass me by. The dogs are sleeping in the back grateful for the air and I think a little happy to be out of the small room that they were spending a lot of time in at Kathy's place. Did they know that we were just starting our trip? Did they realize that we were going to many new places and meeting new and wonderful folks? Did I know this?

CHAPTER 3
TENNESSEE AND DEVLIN

Layers. This trip was about trying to find myself. I had buried the real me under layers upon layers. It was safer to become dormant than to take on the deeds that I had done to get here. I am taking on these fears one by one so that I don't allow fear to run my life. It can only take over your self if you allow it.

Reconnecting with Devlin allowed some of those layers to be shed. It felt so good to hang out and discuss where we have been. I didn't fail him as I thought I did. He took responsibility of his own life and he understood that I tried to help him the only way I knew how. Yes, I was tough but he knew that. He knew that I was doing it for him.

"Get out of bed your supposed to be going to school now."
"I don't want to I'm tired" he slurs from under the blanket
I don't care if you are tired you have 3 more credits to do in math and then you graduate. What the hell are you doing lying around and losing this opportunity?"
I don't care. I just don't. I hate math and I can't do it."
"You are making a choice here Devlin. You know that you can do it. It is hard but don't let one class stand in your way."
"Whatever" and he rolls over and hides under the covers.
What am I supposed to do? I have used water on him, I have asked his friends to help. He is almost a grown man and I can't force him to go. I could drag him into the car and then drop him off at school but I know he wouldn't go in school. As soon as I drive away, there he would be headed to the mall. This is beyond me.

....I lie awake listening to the sounds of night creep into the room. It is past midnight and I still lie here in a suspended state, waiting for the sounds of the bike to bring closure to the day. I can hear the clock strike one and he still isn't home. Wait, is that the rumble of noise that I need to hear? Yes, I can hear the bike as he decelerates for the turn. Now it fades as he goes around the corner and the trees absorb the noise. There it is again as he hits the flats, I turn over and finally let sleep take me as he comes down the short expanse of our road. He is home; he is safe. One more long night is over. Not all nights end like this. More do than not, but there are nights that I lie awake until the call comes. I grab for the phone in the dark and hope that it is his voice that I will hear not a stranger's.

"Yes, I can come pick you up. Where are you? Yes, where are you keys?" I sigh as I put the phone down. I get my clothes on and load up the dogs and we head into the night to get Devlin home.

..."I can't take this anymore. I need for you to move into your own place"
"Your kicking me out?"
"Yes, I can't take the waiting and the constant Unknown of if you are coming home on the bike in the truck or in an ambulance. I can't handle it any more. I will help you try to find a place but I just can't do this anymore."
"Whatever!"
He moved to an apartment in Burlington and I saw him randomly. We would get together to walk the dogs but not much contact was going on. He then hooked up with a girl and he moved away. I tried to get in touch with him through his dad. I sent my New Year letter to his dad and told him to call me. I wanted to see him or talk to him. Nothing.

Then...

I woke up and checked my phone. It was Sunday and I thought I would call Tiny or Lorna to go out for breakfast. I turned it on and it said that I had three messages. Ok.

I listened to the first one.

"I know it is late and you are sleeping but answer the damn phone. Pick up would you." I listened to it at least three times and I couldn't figure it out? Who the hell is this?

" I was up late last night and I was talkin to friends and I was talking about how much I missed Worf and how much I miss Baxter. I miss them, dammit. Wake up. I know that you can hear the phone, wake up. Call me"...

Ok, who the hell is this... I can't figure it out. I thought to myself. I looked at the phone and recognized that there are two text messages too. No one texts me. I look at the phone as I go through the motions to figure out how to get to the text messages. I haven't used this feature before. *Call me. D* shows up on the phone. D? Who the hell is... Oh my god is that Devlin? I look at the next text. Here is my number... call me Devlin... Yes, Yes... it is him. I look down at the phone and I start hitting the letters to text him back.

Dude, call me when you wake up. I am here. I was sleeping and the phone was off. Call me anytime. I then called him and left the same message.

"Hey guess who called me last night?" I asked Tiny.

"I have no idea"

"Devlin. Of course he was drunk and I couldn't figure out who it was until I looked at the text he left but it was him. Can you believe it?"

"Where is he?" she asked.

"I don't know he hasn't called me back. Can you believe it. It's been like 8, 9 years. Wow"

I waited all day and nothing. I know that he sleeps late. And, yes, he called me at 2 in the morning so maybe he slept real late but it is 3 in the afternoon. Dang! I am calling him. I waited as the phone rang, rang. Click.

"D- how the hell are you? This is Maria. I'm sorry I called you so late but I was with these friends of mine and we got to talking about dogs and I kept telling them about Worf and Baxter. How Baxter would always just look at me that way he did and you knew he was talking to you. You know. And I had to call you. I'm sorry it was so late."
"That's fine. Where are you?" I asked him.
"I'm in Tennessee living in my father's house."
"How did you get my number?" I asked him.
"Well I was with my friends and after they left I searched for the letter that you sent my father and I found your number. And I called." And that's how we reconnected. It was laughter and joking from there on as we caught up on times past.

"Why don't you come up and help me get the house and farm together before I go? I will pay for your flight and you can work it off by doing some hard labor for me."
"No, I can't do that."
"D- I want to see you. It will be great. We can go for walks with the dogs and you can do me a big favor in helping me get everything done so I can leave without worrying about the farm."
"I will think about it"

In the end he did come up and we enjoyed time spent on the porch watching the fire flies wink at each other and the sun set behind the trees. It was great to reconnect and just sit and talk as two adults. We decided that I would head to Tennessee to see him since I was going to South Carolina with Angie on the first leg, so why not head to see him. His place was about 6 hours from the first stop on my trip just a little hop compared to the long leaps I was going to take on this trip.

Early morning dew drips from the honeysuckle. I hear the muted sounds of birds as they flitter through the morning mist. I can see the golden light of the sun reflected in the fields below me. The dogs leave tracks as they walk among the mist. The heavy dew reminds me of a light snow. I keep expecting a deer to walk out of the mist but all I am graced with are birds. There doesn't seem to be any large animals here. I forget that I am surrounded by suburbia. I miss my woods. The day begins. So here we are after 8 years of silence. I think we fall into a routine that fits quiet well. I get up early and walk the dogs in the cool of the morning. Well it isn't cool but it is at a point that we can go for an hour walk and only have to stop once for Raven. I get back and Devlin is up. We cruise around looking at sites and then we get back after a day out and he cooks for us. Or we had some kind of food associated with the South. Can't do much better.

"Hmm smoking again? Do you get up and that is all you think of?"

"Pretty much."

"Guess I will leave that alone. I just don't understand how you can willingly kill yourself. But hey that is your decision. So we go to the Smokeys' today?"

"Yeah, was thinking we go up to this great trail that I brought Dad to. It was pretty and then we can go to Cade's Cove."

"Sounds good to me"

"I'm driving right?" He asks with a wicked grin.

"Yeah, whatever. I will be driving for weeks so it will be good to let you drive. You know the way anyway, so I can yell at you to stop when I need to take a picture. Right?" He smiles and agrees. I usually don't let folks drive. I have such a control issue but I know that it makes him feel complete to be behind the wheel. I can't even imagine him stuck in the car without anything to do but wonder when the next time we are going to stop so he can get out and have a cigarette. What is it like to have such an addiction?

We spent all day in the Smokey Mountain Forest and I take some great pictures but it is silent. I crawl into small spaces to capture a waterfall and I am alone in the dense greenery.

Where are all the birds? If I was doing this in Vermont, I would be eyeballed by at least a few ground birds and I am sure there would be few who would be very pissed that I was so close to their nests. I look up and try to find the little warblers that make their home in the canopy in Vermont. Nothing. It is eerie, and I don't understand it. The woods here are beautiful. It does remind me of home except for the bursts of color from the rhodies that find their home in some of the rocky outcrops.

It is warmer with a heavy feeling in the air, too. It should make everything green like home but there isn't as much undergrowth here. It is more open and I can see the ground cover. In Vermont the dense ferns and shrub layers hide the ground from watchful eyes. Here it is green but not the many hues of home.

We are driving out of Cade's Cove when there seems to be a traffic jam out of nowhere.

"What the...." says Devlin. I look around to see if there is anything that we should be looking at but all I can see are people in their cars. We start to crawl forward and then I see folks getting out of the cars with their cameras and creeping up along to the right.

"Um I am going to see what they are looking at ok?"

"Sure," Devlin replies. "Figure out if it is worth stopping." I get out of the car and proceed up the line of idling cars that are creating a parking lot on this small rural road. I come upon the group of peepers and look up to where they are pointing and notice a black shape sort of moving in jerky motions. I bring my camera up to my eye and zoom in. Oh now that is worth getting out of the car. It's a black bear scratching as it sits on its butt and leans on an old tree. I snap off a few pictures but it is so far up the hill and there is so much vegetation that it just looks like a black mass, not much definition. I sure would have to explain this picture if I was going to share it. I took some video and that looks more like a bear but not really. I head back to the jeep that is now about 10 paces closer and get in.

"Well what was it?" Devlin asks.

"It's a bear that is very itchy. I can't get a good picture because it is leaning up against an old log and way up the hill."

We head slowly along as folks figure out that they aren't going to get a good picture and the line of cars starts to amble passed the gawkers.

It is about 10 minutes past the time of the last sighting and another line of cars seems to be stopped.

"What now, another black spec in the woods?" I sarcastically ask.

"Oh just get out and go look " Devlin replies. "Its not everyday you see a black spec in Vermont."

"Hmm." I mumble as I jump out of the jeep and walk over to the mob.

I do see another bear and this one is close. It is across the road and sniffing along a stream. It is sort of cute because I can actually hear it sniffing. It picks up its head and looks about at all the folks with their cameras and seems to just shrug. It ambles across the road and now it is much closer. I duck behind the jeep and start the video on my camera. It shuffles through the ferns and keeps heading my way. I keep the jeep in between me and it but it starts to get within twenty feet and I start to worry about the dogs in the car. They haven't seen it but I can imagine Bristol's response when he does see it. Raven is not likely to pick up her head so I don't have her to worry about.

The bear now passes the jeep and I tell Devlin to make sure the window on that side is shut. It keeps heading my way so the ranger that has shown up tells everyone to get in their cars. Yup, that is where I am headed.

I jump in and shut the door and at that moment Bristol sees the bear. He bounces up and lets out a deep bark as he stiff legged the door. "Bristol, that is enough" I yell at him even though I am laughing, because the bear doesn't even pick his head up.

"Oh god we're all goin to Die." Devlin mumbles as I laugh and pat him on the back. "That's a big son of a bitch" he says as he starts to put up his window. I keep laughing and filming and the bear obliviously wanders farther away.
"Did you get that on film?" I ask as the bear gets too far to film.
"Yeah,I did."

"Are you hungry?" Devlin asks.

"Yes. We just drove for an entire day and you ask me if I am hungry?"

"Gotta take you some where. You are going to love this and I am sure you will be hooked."

"Ok, so what is it."

"Sonic. It has these great burgers and the best frozen slushies. It is so cool, you just pull up to the speaker and order and they bring your food out like the old drive-ins."

"Sounds great I am so hungry."

We drive in and I love the décor. It is decked out like the old drive-ins. "This is cool. Do they come out to your car?"

"Yeah,I told you, they bring your stuff and then you pay them."

The ever present miser... "Do you tip them?"

"I don't very much." He sheepishly grins.

"Yeah but is that because it is Devlin's rule, or we aren't expected to tip them?"

"Hell if I know."

While we wait Bristol hangs his head over the barrier and looks at us.

"Look at the big man... just waitin for the food," Devlin observes. "Its like he knows what a drive in is"

"Well, of course, he can smell the food and why would we be waiting here if it wasn't for food."

"Good point."

While I was in Colorado it was a daily thing. Did it bring me closer to Devlin or was it that they were pretty cheap and it was a good way to stay hydrated? You tell me.

I spent a little longer than a week with Devlin. I kept telling myself that I would go the next day and then I would say that the next day. It was so comfortable to be hanging with him and I felt like it was good for the both of us. We would talk and walk with the dogs. He would play ping pong with his friend that stopped by and we would reminisce about what was, and how fun the times past were. It was good to just be with him. But eventually I had to get on my way. I had a date with a hotel in Hot Springs Colorado and I didn't want to push the time too close.

On the day I left he cleaned the car and insisted on making sure that everything was in tip top shape. It was nice to be fussed about. I had seen a little owl that he had made from a few walnut shells and he said he would make one for me. We had walked on this nice green way in Maryville one night and we picked up some new shells so he could make me one for the trip. When I would go to bed he would stay up late working on the little owl and listen to his music as one of the night bugs he was. He hadn't changed.

"Call me when you get to Kentucky, ok?" Devlin was hanging in the car as I was ready to leave.
"Yeah. I will make sure that I keep in touch. And you too! No more of this disappearing for eight years. Ok? I really enjoyed the time spent here with you. It is what I needed before I headed out on my own." He smiled and pushed away from the

jeep. "You take it safe." I pulled away and there was Tennison sitting on the dash. He would watch as the miles sped under the roof of the jeep and the terrain changed. And he would be there as I changed and found my soul in the one place I forgot to look. Myself.

CHAPTER 4

KENTUCKY:
CAMPING 101

I'm alone. I have traveled down the east coast with Angie, spent time in Tennessee with Devlin and now it is my first night alone.

I end up in the land-between the lakes in Kentucky. I drove around the camp-ground a couple of times to familiarize myself with the area and to find a spot that was not near others but not isolated. It takes me a short time to throw out the dog bed for Raven, so she can settle and I figure out how I'm going to put the tent up. I put it up on the platform with the picnic table. Too many acorns on the ground for me to clean up and it isn't exactly level. So I rig the tent with bungee cords attached to the railing and hang up the fly with more bungee cords and a few leashes to make sure it is over the tent and the water can run off, if it does rain. I put the clean dog beds in the tent and decide to take a nap. After the short nap we walk around the campground and make up some dinner. It was a long day driving and I want to see how the dogs are going to settle in the tent. It <u>Is</u> our first night under the stars.

Oh to the peace of camping, quiet woodland noises, rustle of leaves…NOT here. The red necks are yelling at their kids and the cops are doing drive by's, what have I got myself into?

Journal Entry:
Wednesday:
Left Devlin's and traveled via interstate to Nashville then stopped here in Kentucky. I am at Barkley state park resort. They have a golf course, soccer field and a great beach. The dogs played on the beach but the water was warm, even tepid when I touched it this evening.

The dogs didn't care, they were excited to be on long lines playing in the water and out of the car! The campsite has lots of kids but they are reasonably quiet. The campsite looks over the lake and is wooded. Nice with a breeze. The chiggers are still bothering me on my legs but I guess it was worth the memory ☺ Will miss Devlin. He was fun to be around. He kept my attitude positive. I have Tennison. The little owl Devlin made for me. He sits on the dash board, very cute. Going to read and then hit the hay early. Will miss Devlin's "cookin".

Email him... miss cooking and positive attitude

I wake to the sound of water dripping on the tent. Is it rain? I don't hear the rain? I look out to see morning mist dripping from the oaks above my head. The squirrels are scampering back and forth among the trees with nuts in their mouths. Yikes, can't let the kids out of the tent just yet. Need to get the long lines for sure. I can just see Bristol looking up and chasing the dang squirrel as it does its aerial acrobats right through someone's campsite. Not the best way to greet the folks in the next campsite. I feed the dogs and decide to head out. I forget that it is an hour earlier than what my watch says (6am) so it is only 5 am. I pack up, and in the silence of the morning I appreciate being outside surrounded by trees and nature. I don't see or hear anyone else in the crowded campground getting up or even using the bathrooms. I start the car and load everything and everyone in. I decide to walk the dogs on the beach away from the campground so I head for the beach parking lot.   Well, we were so early the gate wasn't open for the beach so I turned around and thought I headed to the exit. But all I found were locked gates. What? I can't leave until the Ranger comes back? Oh, well, guess I need to hang out for a while so I found a parking lot that looked like it was going to be along the lake and we walked down the hill through the woods in the general direction of the beach.

The kids find a log to play with and I sit there watching the bugs skim across the water. It is peaceful. We walk back to the car and on the way pass Canada geese in the parking lot. They were the only ones there besides the dogs and me. We get back to the car and I decide to try to leave again. It has been at least an hour so I think the gate might be open now. I head out and notice that I had taken a wrong turn, the gate was open all the time. Jeesh, what a green horn to this traveling thing I am. I had taken the road to the beach. Of course it was closed. It was 5 in the morning. I sat in the car and wondered if this was going to be a trip of learning experiences and growth or a very long and arduous trip of one mistake after another. ☹

I'm not excited about the trip yet. I am just getting into the groove of traveling alone with the dogs and the camping thing is still real new. I embrace the driving though, and take back roads mostly and leave the interstates to the trucks and the locals wanting to get from point A to point B. I don't really have a destination except the signs need to keep saying WEST.

CHAPTER 5

MISSOURI
MEMORIES OF TIMES PAST

As I left Kentucky, I was excited. I was on the road and I was happy. I can actually do this. The dogs and I were successful in setting up camp, eating and then taking down the tent. We were enjoying ourselves. I hadn't known if that was going to really happen. I had this dream for so long that I didn't know if it could really come true. I didn't know if the dream was and only could remain in my head. Could I drive across this continent and have fun and learn something about myself? I wanted this. I wanted it to become real. My imagination was in over drive and I hoped that what I was about to experience was going to live up to the pictures in my mind.

I think of my uncle as I hit the Missouri state line. I miss the times that we spent during the fall at my Uncle and Aunt's in Connecticut. Whenever I smell the damp earth and the bright leaves that litter the ground, I think of spending time at Aunt Maureen and Uncle Glenn's. The house, that smelled of home cooking and was always full of people, was one of my favorite places to go. It meant that we were away from my grandmother and I could run outside and play. My aunt and uncle lived where I wanted to. Their house was in the country, surrounded by fields and a pond. I lived on concrete and sidewalks. It was great fun there. My uncle would take us out on walks and we could just sit outside or when we got older we could play in the pool. I still remember swimming with his pet raccoon in the pool. Now that was living, I thought. My uncle was from the Missouri hills. He was a tough nut and built like the old times. Broader than he was tall. His skin was always bronzed from working out in the sun and he had a booming voice. He was mostly quiet though. You didn't mess with Uncle Glenn. The Germanos' were the Wee folk compared to the Pughs. There were five kids and not one of them was small. They all looked like they were brought up on the farm. Now us Germanos, skinny little city kids come out to visit the country cousins. It was sort of funny really.

"Hey, Germano, hand me those peanuts," Uncle Glenn would say.
"Where are they Pugh? I can't find them," my dad remarks his hands swing along the table.
"To your right." My dad would find the nuts and then pass along the bowl. They would sit there for hours and I don't know what they would talk about but that nut bowl would get passed back and forth between them at regular intervals.

   I drove the secondary roads and then hit I-70. It was almost straight and I hit the cruise at 62 (I figured out when I had the GPS on that it was actually 60, but I didn't know that for a long time). I had figured out on the way to Kentucky that if I set it at 62 then good ole Blue got the best gas mileage.   Missouri was hot, and by the time I was looking to settle it was in the high 80's. I looked on the map and found a park that wasn't far from the highway and took the exit. I got to the gate and drove around looking at the sites. The sign said to set up camp and then come and use the drop box for the fee. I drove around the loop and chose a shady spot. I took the dog bed out and Raven settled right in. I got the dog food ready and fed them. We walked around the park since I had my choice of sites and I wanted to see where the most level sight was. It was hot. We walked around for about 15 minutes and I noticed Bristol looking back at me a few times. Uh oh, and Bristol proceeded to give back his dinner. Ugh... ok maybe it is too hot.

I decided to get back in the car and get back on the road. I wasn't feeling all that comfortable being alone at the camp with only the host there. Guess it was safety in numbers for me. I was still new at this and felt it. Bristol was hungry again and I figured if I got back in the car his stomach would settle with the air on so I decided to drive a little longer. There was another park a little down the way and it would be later and then I might find others stopping for the night. As I was getting the supplies back, a real weird bug was sitting on the spare tire. I had no idea what it was. Ok that's it... I am going to head out. It was funny that the weird bug really made the decision clear for me. Why? I still can't figure it out?

We headed back to I-70 and there not fifteen minutes down was a bright billboard saying $45 dollars a night for a new motel six. I knew that they had a pet policy so I pulled off and hoped for the best. It would be great to spend a night in a hotel for the dogs... it was way too hot for them. I drove down the ramp and noticed a Mc D's. Well, why not? I am in a hotel so why not go all out and have fast food. I got up to the drive in window and noticed that they had happy meals with the characters from Ice age. Hmm

"Can I take your order?"

"Yes, what toy is in the happy meal this evening?" I ask politely.

"There is the squirrel toy in it, you know the little one that runs around in the movie."

"Ok, I will have a cheeseburger happy meal with a sprite please."

The woman then told me the total and I headed around the building to get my meal and most importantly my little Scrat. I thought that Tennison would love a pal and he and the little guy could take up shop on the dash together. Ah, what a night, air, fast food, and snoring dogs.

We settled in and I put the air down to 62 and the dogs were out snoring in minutes. They didn't move all night. I even had to coax them out to go to the bathroom at around 9. Guess they appreciated the bed and the air. It was only the first week and they were happy to be in a bed with cold air blowing on them. I hope we are going to make it. I laid down and watched tv. I hadn't seen tv in two weeks. I flipped through the channels not really seeing anything. Didn't take me long to shut it off and snuggle under the covers.

We were off early in the morning. I had spoken to a Esmond dog owner that was on the same list serve as I and she invited me to her house. It was a tempting offer to eat a meal in a house and have a roof over my head. It hadn't been long since I was at Devlin's but it felt good to reach out to a fellow dog owner and see that even though she didn't know me she was offering her house and a meal. There really are good people out there. This country was built on partnership and looking out for those in need and in her small way she was helping me. This trip's purpose was to find who I was and in that I wanted to know others.

It was over cast when we left and the TV had suggested rain so I wasn't too upset to be sleeping in a house when we got down to it. As I drove to meet her at a dog show in Missouri, I noticed that the routes were labeled with Letters not numbers like at home. Hmm, weird. How would you keep track of the north and south, like the odds being east west and the evens being north south? Wonder what their scheme of things is here? As I covered the miles and it started to rain, I thought of my Uncle Glenn. He had grown up in Missouri and then moved north with the Navy and settled up there with my Aunt. These were the people I identified with in my mom's family. They were good people. Hard working and who enjoyed the outside for what it was.

My Uncle was tough and he used to bring me out on walks and we would talk trees and squirrels and all the other things we would pass as we crept through the woods. He was the one who took me out "hunting." Ok, we never shot anything but he and I would walk through the woods with gun in hand and quietly sit alone together enjoying the play of light through the trees. He would take me out on the pond near the house and we would catch frogs. He would laugh when I would run after Tiny with them as she screamed "Ma" at the top of her lungs. I felt kinship with him. He understood how to just sit in the woods and enjoy what Mother Nature was giving us. He was a little crazy like me. He used to hang glide and went all over the country when he was younger to drop off the "best" cliffs. We all thought he was just a little nuts. I loved him for the adventure in him though.

He was the one who showed me how to run a snow machine and he would take me all bundled up in the snowsuit, barely able to move it was so tight and we would scream across the corn fields in the snow. After being so contained in the grasp of the city, it was wonderful. It was where I thought I belonged. It was so hard to get into the car and head back to Massachusetts. I wanted to stay in the country. That was my home.

All these thoughts and more flitted through my mind as I drove on through Missouri to reach the dog show and a new

friend. This is what this trip is all about isn't it? Opening up
myself to the open road and seeing where it takes me.

   Oh, Missouri! No amazing picture opportunities, no desire to
come back, but it did spark lots of childhood memories.

CHAPTER 6
KANSAS

YOU SOMETIMES NEED TO BE SURROUNDED BY NOTHING TO FEEL SOMETHING.

I am back on the road after spending some time with Lisa, her husband and her dogs. It was good to meet positive and fun folks on the trip. It was good to be in a home, too. I was headed West without much planning. I was going to try to head across Kansas as fast as possible because I wanted to get to Colorado. My reservations were not for two more nights but I thought maybe I could travel farther north and

then head down to Colorado Springs. I started to drive through farm country. I was leaving the rolling hills of Missouri and the trees for open prairie. It looked great. It was over cast as I pulled into a rest area to walk the dogs and stretch my own legs. There seemed to be a real cool kind of sculpture at the top of the hill of the rest stop so I headed up hoping that there was a path all the way up. There was a cool winding path that did lead up so I was able to see my first vistas of the wide open prairie. At the top I took some pictures of the sculpture that was there to honor the first windmills that pulled up water for the crops. I could see hawks on the currents of air that swirled around me and I took my first pictures of the prairie that I would soon fall in love with. I didn't realize how amazing the open sky was because the clouds were so low but little did I know that I would long to lift my hands to the sky and feel my soul reach out to the sun and I would feel free and at peace.

I drove into Selina and took a secondary road to the park that was on my map. It was the 4th of July and I wanted to get to the state park early enough to make sure that I could get in. I drove down the road that was so straight I could see for miles ahead. This was my first experience driving on a road that I could see for miles and miles and not be a super highway. Was all of Kansas like this? Yeah, it was. Anyway, I hoped that my trusty map would take me to the park. It was a little desolate out here. I hadn't passed a human habitation in about 30 minutes. Having traveled most of my adult life in New England and on the east coast, I was a little uncomfortable being out where I hadn't seen any sign of humans in a long time.

I finally saw some signs that confirmed my map and I smiled a little more as I crept towards my destination. It was supposed to be a lake created by a dam but I couldn't see anything that was telling me there was a dam ahead. I was used to huge structures that were snuggled in between rocky outcrops, holding back the fast rushing streams of New England. Oh, yeah, I was in Kansas. There are no rocky ledges of bedrock. I was almost there when I saw the dam ahead of me. It was a long low hill. Ha, that's funny. I made my way across the "dam/hill" and followed the signs to the state park. I pulled in to the shack at the gate and there were two adorable elderly ladies, sitting back in beach chairs knitting. It was only three in the afternoon so I was hoping that there was space.
"Hi, I was wondering if you still had space for the evening?"
"Sure, just drive around and then come back with the site number."
"Thanks, I have dogs, is that ok?"
"Oh yes. You just need to keep them on leash."

"Thanks."

Yeah, that's right. It was the middle of the week. I was in the mid west not crazy Patriotic New England. The area that I just drove to get here was almost devoid of people for at least 40 min. Yeah, guess it just didn't get crowded around here. I found a good spot near the water with open campsites all around me, and the bathroom only about 100 yards away.

I got back to the hut and waited for the ladies to notice I was standing there.
"Hi, here is the number of the campsite." I said as I gave them the little card from the post that I had collected.
"You won't be able to see the fire works from there," one of them said.
"That's, ok, I will probably be in bed by the time they go off." They just smiled and gave me my change and I left with the dogs to go for a walk before I set up camp.
The sunset was amazing... colors and the sun sank into the horizon so slowly without any obstructions. While the sun set,

the dogs and I enjoyed playing in the water and watching the locals splashing in the water with their own kids. I really did open my heart to this area. This was the first place I could start to experience the skin peel away from the long held covering over my heart. I could feel the blood start to seep into the spaces that I had closed off for so long. It really felt as if I could open my body to the sky and let some of the weight just float away.

Journal Entry:
4th of July and sitting in the tent. Traveled to Kansas and loved the wide open spaces and big sky. The dogs had fun playing in the water and I took great sunset pictures. Lots of fire-works and it was 86 degrees but not so humid.

    I left the campground in the morning and it was the first time I left a place that I wanted to look back at, and drive slowly away. I didn't get but 2-3 miles and I wanted to stop and take pictures. This is what I had thought of as prairie for so long in my mind and now I was standing amongst grasses that really did wave in the wind. I stepped out of the car and the dogs and I walked away from the car. I spun in a circle with my hands out and felt the air move across my arms, the sun on my face and the soft sounds of the open fields upon me. My visions of the state couldn't match the amazing reality that surrounded me. My spirit soared above me and I could feel the weight of times past lifting off of me. It was as if some of the hard shell that protected me was blowing away with the wind. I felt the breath leave me and not be contained by the ever present bubble that usually protected me. I lifted my face to the sun and stood still among the waving grass.

I drove on the continuous straight road and looked left and right and felt like I could get lost in the ever present sky. I pulled off on a farm road and turned around so that I could eat lunch on the tailgate and have a 360 degree view. My eyes were the only thing that stopped me from seeing forever. There were no mountains, no trees or buildings to hinder the sky. It was laid out across the horizon inviting me to lose myself in its beauty. I made the decision to stay another night in Kansas as the sky wrapped itself around me and I felt free.

It was as if I was drawn to the open sky. I wanted to continue this cleansing of my heart and body. It was as if this was a step that I needed to take before I could climb into the mountains once again. I needed to let my spirit soar amongst the wispy clouds and the blue of the sky. I needed to have no obstruction to hold it down. I felt as if I were flying.

I drove to the other reservoir with a campground on my map and sat at the beach in the sun with the dogs playing in the water. I had only driven for about 4 hours but I didn't want to leave this sanctuary. I pulled out my chair and wrote in my journal and listened to the waves come ashore. Here in the heart of the country, I could close my eyes and hear the waves lap at the shore. If I just imagined the smell of the sea, I could be there. The comfort I felt as I peered at the vastness of the open sea I could also feel here. Landlocked in the center of the continent I was transported back to the ocean shore and the liberation I felt from the ocean was one in the same, here at the lake amongst the grasses. The cleansing sounds of the waves taking the pain and the darkness back with them into the depths as they reached out to me and then retreated into the deep. Yes, this was the right decision. I felt that I belonged here.

I put up my tent along the shore. I was alone tonight, no kids playing in the water, or families hanging out at the *campfires*. July 5th was not a holiday and it was the middle of the week. Farmers don't get many vacation days and this was in the middle of farm country. I spoke to the folks who were camp hosts when they stopped in to check on me. I was in the process of taking pictures of the moon and we talked for an hour. These were good people. I had traveled half way across the continent and through many different regions and the people had all embraced me. I found solace in the idea that

most who spoke with me had done a similar journey in their lives.

I settled in to the tent and watched as the moon climbed in the sky and created light were there was darkness. I felt as if it was lighting my darkened heart too. I stared up at it as Raven moved against my back and Bristol put his foot over my arm and the last puzzle piece fit together... and I became complete. The light of the moon shone down upon the happy family that was exploring what it was like to be free. *Absolutely free.* I closed my eyes and my spirit lifted and traveled with the moon as she moved across the sky. I felt warm and secure with my kids and I fell into a deep sleep knowing the next day I would be able to fly once more under the uninterrupted sky.

Climbing Closer to the Sky

The peace that I had always felt in the mountains was created by Mother Nature surrounding and protecting me. The different greens and browns of the trees with their branches reaching out to me, the soft whisper of the breeze in the needles and leaves, this is where I felt at home.

I woke early in Kansas and walked the dogs along the shore of the lake. It was amazing to see the blue of the lake in contrast to the skeleton trees. Here once tall trees stood reaching their branches to the sky as their roots sought out the water source of the river moving slowly by them. Now only stark white skeletons remained standing in the man made lake shore. The dogs splashed through the water chasing each other as the sun rose to color the water yellow with its warmth. We walked around for a while so that the dew could burn off the tent and we could be on our way.

I was pretty good at taking down camp now. I could fold and shake out the campsite quickly and my routine helped me get grounded. In no time we were loaded up and pointed West once again. I jumped on the secondary road that lead up to the main highway that would take me to Colorado. I avoided the

big highways because I wanted to see the country, not the back end of trailer trucks. I was amazed again at the checkered pattern of roads here. I took off west and then there was a slow corner and then I was traveling North, and I mean I was traveling north. No bends in the road, no rivers to follow as they cut into the sides of mountains. Wow it was so free here. I watched as I approached a rail yard. It had been abandoned but all the cars were still there lined up in neat rows just as the roads here were. The tracks paralleled the road I was on as I crept slowly to the main highway. The landscape of rows and rows of corn or other crops were interrupted by clumps of trees that hid the farm houses. As I drove past I noticed almost one out of three were abandoned. It was so depressing to drive along and see the beautiful porches leaning to the side with the weight of the years gone by. Alone they stood without anyone there to tell the stories of their past. What a different world here. Even the posts that I drove by were different. They were made from the ground; A type of stone that the settlers had cut to use as posts because there weren't enough trees to use. I had come from a state that was covered by trees, eighty percent of it. Those trees were the settlers building materials, shelter, and food. Here they used what mother earth gave them in a different resource. Human ingenuity and Mother's bounty together.

I sped along the highway and I noticed the landscape changing. It was going from green to a grayish silver. The Kansas prairie was giving itself up to the sage brush of Colorado. It wasn't an abrupt change but as I drew closer to the mountains the colors changed. They became lighter and the green of the rolling grasses changed to small shrubs and open spaces of hard yellow and white earth. There weren't great big signs as there are on major highways so I only knew I had crossed into Colorado when I slowed down for the next town and the little square sign welcomed me to Colorado. It was amazing to see the small towns come into focus in the distance as I scanned for wildlife. There were a smattering of small houses, a gas station, a grain elevator and railroad tracks that I either followed or crossed. That was it. Many of them looked deserted but as I slowed down I could see movement around one or two of the buildings. Now this was roughing it. Ha, folks back at home think it is tough to have the grocery store half hour away. Imagine living here. I hadn't crossed a big town in about an hour or two. Now this is space. Wide open space.

I was on another secondary road that was taking me to Colorado Springs. It was miles and miles of open sage and fences. I pulled off on a ranch road. They had gone from farms to ranches very quickly after I hit the sage. I wanted to take some pictures of the sage up close and the well that I saw. It was so classic. I had to stop. I was the only one on the road so it was easy just to pull off and drive over the cattle guard and turn around. There wasn't another vehicle, building or anything moving as far as the eye could see, and that was far. I was about ten minutes into taking pictures with the dogs wandering around when I saw a semi coming closer. I could tell it was slowing down. Hmm they usually don't slow down. As it approached, I could see that the driver was waving at me. I thought quickly and held up my camera and smiled. He smiled back and threw it into gear and sped up. Yeah, a car stopped out here might need help. Wasn't that nice. It isn't just at home in rural Vermont that folks will lend a hand. Here, so far away from home I am greeted with the same kindness and concern by passersby. It felt good to be noticed by a stranger in this way.

"Ok kids let's go", I called to the dogs and we were on our way.

I was told by everyone to keep looking so you could experience the mountains as they rise up out of the plains before your very eyes. Ok, so I kept scanning the horizon looking and looking. I watched as the ranches got closer and I saw more buildings and people. But no mountains. I looked at the map and I was about 20 miles out from Colorado Springs. I should see the mountains now, right? Nope. I did see some real dark thunderheads and thought maybe they are caught up on the mountain tops. I had to pay attention to the road now because I was going to have to merge to a more heavily traveled road to get to my hotel room. I was trying to get into the correct lane when I looked up and there they were. The mountains. They had been hiding behind the clouds. They were silver and white and grey and, Wow! They were tall. Not the rounded, tree lined ridges of Vermont, but jagged tall and dark. I couldn't see much detail since I was trying to figure out the road to the hotel but it was like they just appeared above me. Naked rock and snow peaked out from the clouds. It was difficult to stay on the road and watch for my exit. I saw the Air force academy come up on my right and I thought of Dusty. I wonder what he is doing now? Will I ever get to see him again and be able to express my emotions to him? I wonder. So many thoughts. Eek! need to pay attention to driving.

Got to the right exit and there it was, Hot Springs Colorado. I had started this part of the trip so long ago when I called and made reservations. I pulled into the information building and went in to ask directions.

"Excuse me I am new to the area and was wondering if you had a relocation package I could have?"

"Yes we have them made up. I will get you one. Are you moving soon?" The elderly gentle man asked.

"Not until next year but I am interested in this area."

"Oh, we have wonderful schools and lots of nice neighborhoods and we are right next to Colorado Springs."

"Yes. Could you tell me where the El Dorado hotel is?"

"You go left out of this parking lot and then it will be down on your right about a mile or so."

"Thanks for the package and the directions. Have a good day." The man smiled and I headed out to the car.

I pulled up into the hotel and it was quaint. Little adobe buildings with Native American stencils on them. Cute, I thought. I got my keys and headed to the little building. I didn't want the one on the road but they said that was the one that they let dogs in so I was sort of stuck. I pulled into my spot and went to go look inside. I opened the door and was greeted with the smell of urine. Oh great. I shrugged and thought that I had seen more hotels around but they all seemed sort of 2nd rate so I knew the price was low and I was paying for it with the smell. Oh well. I got the dogs and we walked around the place a little and I tried to find a green spot for them to walk around on, but it was wall to wall buildings and there wasn't even a side walk. What have I gotten myself into. I was surrounded again. I had just left a place where my spirit was allowed to soar without want and now I was stuck in Seedyville. Ugh.

I took out my stuff and made due. We ate from the cooler and the dogs and I settled in for the night. I crawled under the covers and I wasn't alone on the crawling aspect. There was something crawling on me but I was so tired that I thought I needed a shower and didn't realize what I was in for. I was writing in my journal and scratching at my legs when I finally realized that the crawly things were probably bed bugs. I went to the jeep and got my sleeping bag and pulled the covers back up and hoped for the best. The dogs had a chemical repellent on, so I didn't have to worry about them but I was going to be uncomfortable!!! It was too late to find another spot and I didn't know the area well. Here I was in a hotel and not on the hard ground and more uncomfortable than I had been in days.

The dogs and I got up early and headed out to explore. If I could find a hotel, I would not come back. I packed up everything just in case and we were off. I wanted to explore Colorado Springs and the area around it so I put the directions into the computer and we headed out. As we were driving out, we passed a Sonic. Now I knew where I was going for dinner. Thoughts of Devlin and the fun we had floated around me. I missed that little booger.

I passed really nice neighborhoods as I headed into Colorado

Springs. The computer said turn right and I headed down through a neighborhood that looked like it was planned in Hollywood. It had bungalows that were spaced nicely apart with flower gardens bursting with color. Wow!

As I approached a light, I noticed it said dead end ahead. What? Man the stupid computer was wrong. Dang. I pulled up into the parking lot and tried to figure out where I was. It turned out that I was in the parking lot of a nature preserve and there were hiking trails that I could take the dogs on. Well not bad for a wrong turn. I grabbed the dogs and some bags and we headed out to look for the trails. We were walking away from the lot towards a building when I saw a biker sitting on a bench. His helmet was on the bench next to him and he looked sweaty and a little tired. Ah, a local. Always ask the locals where the best trails are, so I headed over. He didn't look intimidated by the dogs and he had a nice smile. "Hi I am looking for some trails to walk the dogs on, do you know of any?"   "Yeah you don't want to go up the Seven Falls one because you have to pay and they really aren't worth it. You should go up this road and there are trails that parallel it along the stream. It's

hot but the stream is there for the dogs and you can get some great views at the top."

"Thanks. I took a wrong turn and ended up here so guess I can try it. The dogs and I are tired of being in the car so it will be a good change."

"Are you on vacation?" He asked.

"Yeah, I am looking to relocate and Colorado Springs is on my short list."

"I moved here from Texas and I love it."

We talked about the positives of Colorado and how he hated the heat in Texas. The folks here were real nice and we both agreed that it was a good place to stay in shape.

"I'm a manager of a local grocery store but I wanted to take classes to become a personal trainer and nutritionist, but I just can't find the time."

"Well, there is no time like the present. You shouldn't put your dreams on hold. That's what I did for so long in trying to take this trip. One thing held me back and then it was another and then it was years until I finally decided that what was holding me back wasn't the sick dog or the elderly parents it was me. So here I am going across this

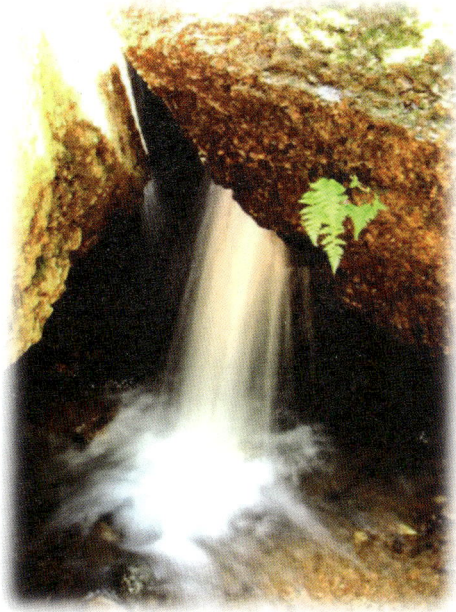

continent and looking for my future. You should do it. Folks want to feel good about themselves and what is more rewarding than helping them feel good?" He smiled at me and I could see he was thinking.

"You know you are right. I should take a harder look at it. Colorado Springs Community College has this program that I looked at a while back and the gym I go to has an internship."

"Well, you should at least try. You seem like a guy who enjoys helping folks. I'm a teacher and it is so rewarding to see kids work out a problem and then see the light in their eyes when they realize that they did it on their own. They solved the problem or they came up with an idea of their own. It's what keeps me teaching." His smile made me feel good to have stopped and talked with him. "Hey it's getting hotter and I need to get going before it gets too hot to walk the kids. Thanks for the heads up about the trails. Good luck with your decision."

"Good luck finding a place to settle. It is great here. Parks and lots of green space and the folks are nice." He smiles when he says that.

"Take care." I say as the dogs and I head up to the trailhead he mentioned. You can always find a kindred spirit if your spirit is open to feel the others out there. It's the opening up part that is the difficult part of the trail not the trail itself.

The dogs and I spend almost all day at the nature preserve walking the trails and taking pictures. At the top I could see Colorado Springs and far beyond. It was amazing to be surrounded by red rocks and evergreens. It was the beginning of my journey in the high desert. I hadn't found any other hotels in the area and I was exhausted from the heat and the sun so we spent another night in the creepy crawling hotel. In the morning I took a shower and packed up. I decided I wasn't going to stay here another night!! I had little red welts on my wrists because they were sticking out of the sleeping bag. Hmm, fleas or bed bugs? I didn't care I was out of here!! I went to the office and waited patiently as they were talking to another customer. "Hi, I am in 7 and I need to leave early. I have paid for three nights but I am not staying ."

"Well you have reservations for three nights so you will have to pay for three."

I was trying to save these folks some face but if they are going to push it, oh well. The people who had just paid were looking at the brochures behind me so I said in a not so quiet voice. "Well there are two large stains on the floor that smell like urine and there are either fleas or bed bugs in the bed." I have the red welts to prove it. Would you like to see them?" I started to lift up my sleeves to show her.

With a look behind me she said "Um, no we will only charge you for the two nights, and we will check out that room for you. It is the room that we allow dogs in it so..." I didn't let her finish the sentence "I don't care if it is the one you put people with dogs in. I travel with my dogs but I expect as nice accommodations as one without dogs. My dogs are well behaved and trained and they would never go to the bathroom in the room. They have a pesticide on them so I am not worried about them. The bugs went after me. I was uncomfortable all night " I said a little louder than necessary. She looked around quickly and her slight nervousness was ramping up a bit after that. I assumed that the folks behind me were listening now so I smiled at her and asked for a discount on the nights I did spend.
"Sure, I can charge you half, would that be satisfactory?"
"Yes, Thank you."

I left and on the way out I smiled at the folks there and picked up three bagels and some coffee to go. I was going to take this place for anything I could after that horrible night. It was still early but I was eager to leave the little hacienda so I loaded up the dogs and we headed towards the mountains. I needed to get away to smell the clean air and remove the weight of the building from my shoulders. I was under a roof for two nights and I started to feel the weight of my life again. I needed the sky to open up for me and soon. As I was leaving, I passed the same Sonic and I was reminded of Devlin and a smile crossed my lips.

We headed up into the mountains with me rubbernecking as we climbed away from the red rocks of Hot Springs to the jagged tightly packed hills of the next town. We actually ended up in Green Mountain Pass. The dogs and I hiked up a trail behind the houses lining the canyon. It was very steep and the dogs and I struggled to just get up to the trailhead. It was a single track and there were lots of signs about mountain lions but I let Bristol run ahead because he would constantly check

in. He didn't get out of sight at all. Raven took up her position in the rear and we headed out for a good hour walk. It was different than yesterdays hike. The trees were closely packed and the hillside was covered in yellow stone and lichen. It wasn't like the red sandstone of yesterday's canyons. We crossed two streams and there were nice waterfalls that the dogs played in. It was steep going but Raven and I tried to keep up with Bristol as best as we could.

I liked the views but I felt so contained like I was hemmed in by the mountains. The sides of the canyons were close and too steep to sit and look out. I needed to get back into the open. I felt like I just had the experience of letting part of my shell crack and open to feel the wind and the air and now I was being held back by the closeness of the mountains. I was restless here.

At the base of the trail we had to cut through a neighborhood that was at the bottom of the canyon and the houses were nice but right on top of each other. If

I wanted that I could have stayed in Hot Springs or Vermont for that matter. No, I wanted to feel the wind and the sun on my face again. We hurried to the car hoping that we would see the sky once we headed up the road.

We left Green Mountain Pass and ended up in Woodland Park. I drove slowly through and saw an amazing building as I crept from light to light. Wow! I need to check that place out. We pulled into the parking lot and the building turned out to be the library. It had huge windows that looked out on Pikes Peak and the sky beyond. Now that is something. There were sections of the foundation that had rocks dedicated to the folks who helped make the library possible. I could live in a community that put architectural pride into their library. I walked the dogs around a little and we saw the sign for the chamber of commerce so I put the kids back in the car and put up the sun screen and headed back to the little square building that promised some tourist help.

I walked in and felt the cool of the air conditioning. Whew, I didn't realize how hot it was outside. I need to make sure I get back to the dogs quickly. There were a few folks behind the counter so I headed over.

"Hi, I am looking at relocating to this area. Do you have a packet or someone who can answer some questions for me?" I asked.

"Hi, let me help you with a relocation package and then if you still have questions I can try to help. Here, June, can you reach under the counter and pull out one of the bags we just put together. Now because she is here personally we don't need to charge her. OK?" The woman talked to the young girl that was helping her. "Now this will have all the usual stuff in it and some flyers to help you get an idea of the place. We have our newspaper in there too so that you can get some local flavor. We are redoing the store fronts this summer and we are excited to see how they turn out." She was genuinely enthusiastic as she told me this information. I thought that maybe she was new to the job and she liked folks.

" So what can you tell me about Woodland Park. I am a teacher and a dog trainer so I am looking for a community that is dog friendly and is interested in its youth."

"Oh you will love Woodland Park then. We are dog friendly and we have a wonderful educational facility with a magnet charter school for math and science. Are you looking to move this year?"

"No, I am looking to move in a year or two and I don't know if I will teach when I get here but I am interested in that amazing library. I could live in a community that created a building like that."

"Yes ,we are very proud of the library. It is an amazing structure."

We continued with our conversation drawing in the young woman who was helping her and the gentleman behind the other counter. We talked about youth and how wonderful and difficult they are. We laughed as the young woman had to support her peers and we all good naturedly assured her that if it wasn't for her and her peers we wouldn't stay young trying to keep up with them.

" Thanks so much for your help and it was great to meet all of you." I said as I prepared to leave.

"Why don't you take my card and please if you need to use my name do so when and if you apply to the schools here. The principal is one of my close friends and I think he would love to meet you." I gave her a big smile. "Thanks, I just might do that. I enjoyed our conversation. Take care and enjoy the summer," I said, as I left the cool of the air to return to the dogs. I hadn't meant to be so long but the dogs were sleeping and didn't seem upset that I had been gone for so long.

I got back in the car and as I prepared to leave I realized that I could live here. It was open and friendly and those folks didn't even know me but for 20 minutes and they were supportive of me moving to their community. Was it a façade that they put on for tourists or were they truly interested in me? What was it? I didn't know but right there I decided to see if there was a hotel around to take us in for the night. I wanted to see more of this place. I needed to go get more food so I would head to the grocery and check out the locals. I had found that was the best place to see the pulse of the area. To see folks at their normal everyday selves and to see what they were really like. Not the face they put on for the tourists, but the face they wear after a long day at work. After getting supplies at the store we got back on the road. The folks in the chamber of commerce said that the best drive was out to Florissant and Divide and so I headed out that way. I wanted to see the countryside and to feel the space it provided.

Pikes Peak Forest

We were stopped at the dam that created Lake George and Bristol disappeared into the tall grass. "What are you doing B?" I yelled. "Let's go little man. There is a swimming hole right down the path. C'mon." He slowly came out of the grass with something in his mouth. "What you got B?" There in his mouth was a tennis ball. That boy can find a tennis ball anywhere. "Ok, B, you can have it" I said laughing, and we headed to the dam so that I could throw his new found toy. After the dogs had fun playing in the water, I drove up a forest road where I parked the jeep and took a walk with them. It was beautiful with lots of flowers in bloom and the whisper of the wind in the pines. It was hot but we had fun walking along the off road track. I didn't see or hear another human. It was great after the time I had spent in Hot Springs surrounded by people. I needed to free my spirit again. I sat on a rock outcropping while the kids walked around sniffing the holes

and hoping for at least one ground squirrel to pop up. I closed
my eyes and felt the warmth of the sun and started to feel the
freedom of the open woods work its magic on my soul. I
touched the closest tree and felt its harsh bark under my
fingertips and knew that I was close to the Earth here. I slowly
spread my spirit up and out of my body and I could feel the
connections to the sky and rocks and trees. Yes, here I felt as
one, not as a stranger.

   After a while the dogs came back to my spot on the rock

and we continued up the ridge line. It was so nice to wander
around without a direction or focus. It was great for the dogs,
too. I started to run out of water so we headed back to the
jeep. It was a good day, a day that I needed to be able to start
on the road tomorrow. I would be heading off to see another
dog breeder tomorrow and I needed to feel a little more
grounded. I liked to meet strangers and see where our
connections were. I headed back to Woodland Park and the
hotel I had seen on the hill.

   On the way back to Woodland Park, I was at a light in Divide
and there was the sign for the county animal shelter. Hmm

should I stop? I think it would be good to connect with dog folks here. I made the right into the parking lot and headed in. It won't hurt to just look at the pups they have and to meet some volunteers. That's what ran through my head but I was still looking for a small dog. Maybe, just maybe it would be from here. I stopped in and met the shelter director and a couple of volunteers. It was great to talk dog and I came out of the building with a smile on my face. It was good to connect with folks here. I had met a few nice volunteers and got to play with a rescue "russel". I needed the dog infusion.

I stayed that night in a nice no name hotel that was clean, cool and a mile above the rat hole I had just stayed in. The next morning we packed up and headed to Silverthorne to see an Entlebucher breeder that I wanted to connect with about pups. I was researching this breed to see if I really wanted one and while out here I should look up as many breeders as I could. There were only two in the New England area and I had not met one of these little dogs since Switzerland. In my experience with most breeds that have originated in Europe, we Americans usually change the breed for our needs and not necessarily stick to what the original intent was so I wanted to see some dogs that were bred here in the US.

I decided to take the back roads up to the area instead of taking the interstate and boy was I rewarded. I drove through the high hills of Woodland Park and Divide and the scenes that flashed along side of the jeep was great. Open fields filled with wild flowers, distant hills dotted with pines and other evergreen trees. It was beautiful. It didn't prepare me for the vista that opened up before me though when I hit Fairplay.

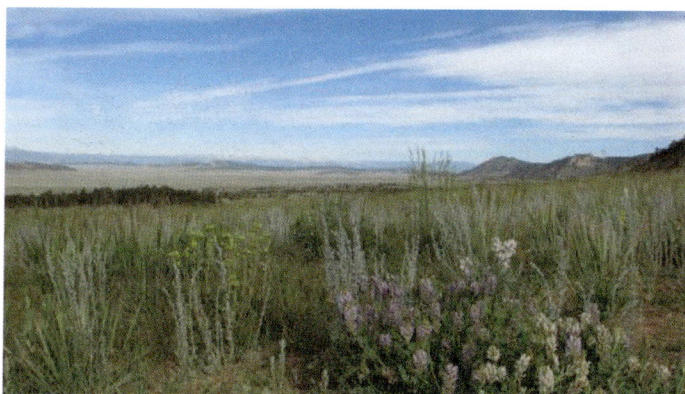

I drove out over a ridge and there laid before me was a wide open plane ablaze in color. It was like a gigantic caldera with a few low hillocks scattered around the center but the feeling it pressed upon me was of space. Wide open space. The hills and mountains that rimmed the area were majestically covered with snow and trees but the flowers, ahh what amazing splashes of color. I slowed down and tried to find a spot to pull over. I found a sandy pull off and got out of the jeep and looked around me. How did this landscape appear to the Native American who first came upon it? Was it filled with elk, mammoths, and horses? I let the dogs out and pulled out my camera and set to work. I wanted to capture this release of color and life that lay before me. It was hard to catch the scope of both because I couldn't find an object to allow the mind to contemplate the space that lay before me.

I snapped away and then loaded up the dogs and headed into the caldera. I swung my head from side to side and even slowed my usual sixty-two down to fifty-five trying to catch all that I could with what limited site my eyes offered me. It was here that I saw my first buffalo. Yes they were in a herd that was clearly managed for food but it was great to see the tall shaggy beast on the side of the road. Not cows or sheep but

Bison!! Yeah... I could now check off that one of my lists of must sees. I continued slowly on my way reaching the foothills of the back range as I crept towards Breckenridge and the place of snow and skis.

I knew I had reached the ski slopes when I saw the log homes start to become log palaces and castles. Oh My! Did they build them big here. I could also tell the wee folk were being taken over by the rich folk because the vehicles changed from the beat up old trucks and SUV's to Mercedes and Lexus'. Yes, I was in money land for sure. I wound around the now steep mountains until I found the house I was looking for to meet Sybil and the pup.

The dogs and I had fun at Sybil's house but it was too steep an incline and economic privilege in this place. We had a nice walk, but it was definitely not my style. Breckenridge made me realize I didn't want that Colorado. I didn't want the Benzes or the Lexus' getting on my butt as I drove my jeep through the town. It was a tourist trap, each condo closer to the next condo. They were all the same. Breckenridge, Silverthorne, Vail. I left that part of Colorado behind and headed west. I couldn't leave fast enough. I wanted the cowboy west not the silver spoon west. You can have it.

If you look hard enough you can see a little bit of yourself in everyone.

I tried to find a campsite in Rifle Colorado but there was a famous cowboy singer and the rodeo was in town so even though I drove 20 miles into the state forest there were

absolutely no campsites available. Ugh, I have to drive 20 miles back out and then head down the highway. Fine. I drove along red and pink sand and stone. It was devoid of plant life and the setting sun put an orange shadow upon the land. The highway was paralleled by large pipes and dotted here and there with these really big fans contained in little sheds. The pipes led toward them but then abruptly went into the ground. I could even hear them with the windows closed and the air going. I wondered what they were. There was really nothing out here, what could they be?

I ended up in Parachute Colorado at a great Holiday Inn Express. I stopped at the first place I could find due to the fact that I didn't see much else on the map. I headed out to walk around the parking lot and down the road a bit. We had walked in Rifle for a while in the canyons before we had do get back on the road, so the dogs were not too full of energy. That was good because there was nothing out here that I could see. Just two hotels, a small Bar-B-Q place and sand. After the evening walk around the group of hotels, I headed for the elevator. I got a tall frozen drink from the free dispenser in the lobby and then the dogs and I squeezed into the small space of the elevator with some fine young men and their brown bags. I think I came up to their waists. Wonder what they are doing here? It seems like there are only men around.

The next morning I went down to breakfast and enjoyed eggs, bacon, and a sweet bun. Much better than the PB and Nutella that was usual morning fair. At breakfast I noticed that there were all men, no women in the breakfast area. The men were either in suits or overalls. Where was I?

"Good-morning" I said to the woman behind the counter as I went to pay for the night.

"Good –morning to ya M'am," said the woman with a southern drawl. She wasn't from around here that was for sure. "I hope your evening was enjoyable".
"Yes, it was thank you. What is around here that the men are all dressed up or look like they belong under a car?"

"You are in oil and gas company land. This here is the only hotel around for miles and there are a lot of workers who got the Friday off."

"Oh, that's why they are so big." I say with a smile.

"Yes, M'am, there are a lot of workers who work in the gas shafts. You will see them as you go along down the highways a bit."

"Thanks. I guess those are the pipes with the fans."

"Yes, the fans are too keep the tunnels cool."

"Oh, they sure are loud." I remark and head out.

As I turned to leave, the gentlemen who was in the manager's room saw the dogs. With a big smile he walked over to them and knelt down. "Well, aren't they beautiful dogs. Can I pet them?"

"Of course, this is Bristol and this little girl here is Raven."

"Oh they are so nice can I get them a treat?" He says as he gets up to go in the breakfast area.

"They would love a treat, thanks," I say as he heads away. He comes back with an entire handful of bacon. "Oh, you need to tell them gentle if you are going to feed them that." I say with a chuckle. He reaches out and Bristol takes one sniff of what is in his hands and the drool just pores out of his mouth. Yummie I can see it in his eyes.

"Gentle, Gentle, here you go big boy" he says as he drops 3 pieces of bacon in Bristol's mouth. "and for the little girl you get an extra one."

"Thanks they haven't had food that good in a long time. We have been on the road for three weeks and that is the best breakfast they have had."

"Where are you coming from?" The man asks.

"I'm from Vermont and we are headed to Washington."

"Have a safe trip and enjoy Colorado"

"Thanks, but I think you just gave the dogs the best taste of

Colorado yet." I say as I smile and head out to the jeep. The dogs and I walk around the hotel looking for a place to stay out of the sun. It has already started to get hot. Bristol pricks up his ears and points in the direction of some low trees. "Hmm what do you hear boy? Ok go see." He trots off and soon I hear a splash and the sound of geese. Leave it up to Bristol to find the only water for miles around.

   The dogs are a little reluctant to go but we head over to the car for our next stage on the journey. We will be leaving Colorado today to head to Utah. It looks like it is going to be a hot one, too.

CHAPTER II
UTAH

Red rocks and tall escarpments fill my view. I feel like I am in a John Ford movie. I crossed into the desert and felt free again.

I found myself on a high plateau with sage and short grasses that seemed to stretch out forever. I could see rock outcroppings in the distance but the land seemed to drop off in the distance. I drove slowly as I had crossed into a landscape that was unfamiliar and I wanted to make sure I wasn't missing anything. It was a naked landscape. It was uniform and not at the same time. I headed off the main highway to take a short tangent to Dead Horse Canyon. It was a state park so they would allow the dogs. In this area around Moab, there were lots of National Parks but I couldn't walk the dogs in those areas so I headed to the park hoping that there would be a space left open for me.

I left the high mesas and started to wind into a canyon with rock outcrops that looked like ships. The walls had strips of color and they rose so high I had to bend my neck to see the top. Oh, I was in Utah all right. I used to see formation like these in books when I was a kid. I would wonder what it would be like to be surrounded by rock and sky, and here I was. In all my travels previously I had not seen the likes of this area. It reminded me of Mesa Verde but there the mesa had been cut with deep crevasse and you had to stand at the edge to see down into the void. Here there were stone and sand formation that stood alone with only the wind to surround them. Wow. I stopped along a pull off and let the dogs out to wander around as I read up on what was before me. I looked about me wondering what else was in store for me and then loaded the dogs up and headed down the road to the park.

I came up on the guard station and slowed down to join the line at the window.

"Hi, are there any more camp sites available?" I asked the ranger.

"I think there is one left, let me check with the ranger at the park. Are you staying more than one night?" she asked.
"No, just the one night." I replied.

"Ok." She picked up a walkie talkie and spoke into it asking if there were any more campsites available. We both waited as there was no response. She repeated the request and then the ranger at the park responded, that yes there was one left. "Do you want to take it" she asked?
"Yes, thanks. Do you want me to pay the entrance fee here?"
" No you can pay when you pay for your campsite."
"Thanks" I said as I pulled away from the station.

It was still a couple of miles to the campsites and as I drove along I got to see the plateau start to break apart and the edges of the mesa pull away from each other. The rocks were red and brown and white. It was so alien to me. I pulled into the ranger station at the campground and paid for my site and headed over. It was in the hundreds and the dogs and I were hot and tired. I set up camp as they lounged under the picnic shelter. I put up the tent but it was too hot to go in there so Raven crawled up on her dog bed and Bristol and I shared the sleeping pad in the little shade that we could find. We all fell

asleep as the heat of the day burned itself out.

I woke to cooler air and a need to check out the area. I loaded up with the water bottle and my camera and the dogs and I set out to explore. I hadn't really looked at the map in too much detail but I knew that there was a trail that went along the rim of the point. We set out on the trail with not much idea what we would find.

The open space swallowed me up in its embrace. Red, all I could see was red. The mountains in the distance loomed up out of the red desert. I was watching the colors come alive as the sun dropped and set the rocks ablaze. I couldn't believe that the color could get more intense than it was, but it became a living flame, flickering red, yellow and white. Blue hills set the warmth of the fire to a thirst. I looked away and noticed some low clouds creeping over the plateau to the west. I could see the rain falling from the clouds but I couldn't feel anything. The rain dissipated before it hit the earth. The red earth. It couldn't be quenched by the rain that fell from the silver clouds hanging above. The shrubs reached up to the sky but for naught, the clouds that were once there were none. It was like I had to turn my eyes away from the intensity of light to be able to truly see what was there. I stared through the small square of my camera to see the entire vista filled with light.

The dogs and I headed around the rim and with each new turn I saw a changing panorama. The sun dropped behind the clouds and the earth changed to grey. It was like someone had dropped a veil over my eyes and the color was gone. I looked behind me to see flashes of lightning and dark clouds. Uh oh. " We need to get going guys." I had been so engrossed in taking pictures of the canyons I hadn't paid much attention to what was going on behind me. "Let's start to head back, Ray and B we need to walk faster." I swiveled the camera to my back and looked at the trail markers. I looked around and figured I was not even half way.

"Ok guys let's cut across this section and hope we pick up the trail on the other side." The dogs looked up expectantly and just smiled. "Let's go." I took a hard right and hoped that the trail would meet up. We weaved through the yucca and small bushes that were scattered in random clumps and we jumped from level to level. It was like Mother Earth had put many layers of cardboard and then bound them together. The force had caused the paper to turn brittle and the edges had fallen away in places. It seems like we were walking up and down, up and down along flat layers of earth. I started to get nervous because this wasn't the land I was used to. In so many places I had gone of trail and always could find my way back. It was like I could communicate with the earth below my feet. It would tell me what way to go. Not here. This was so foreign to me. I didn't feel comfortable. I started to worry.

"Bristol, find home. Find home." He turned and looked at me. His eyes smiled back at me, it was like he was saying, "finally I get to do something". He took a turn to the right and headed off and over the rocky ground. It wasn't but a minute until I heard voices. I looked up and I could see the light pole that marked the campground. I should have told him to find home sooner. He then stopped short and stared down on the small patch of grass under some scrub brush. "Come on B- Let's go." But he wouldn't move. I walked around him and saw the bunny, No, not a bunny, but a hare. It too was still and staring at Bristol. It was big. Wow look at those ears. I slowly took out the camera and tried to take a picture. The light was so grey that I couldn't get any definition but I got it. Bristol and the long eared bugger just stared at each other and didn't move. I took another picture and then turned and dragged Bristol by the leash.

"Let's go Bristol, not for you." He looked longingly at the hare and then walked away. I could tell he definitely did not want to go. Raven came up to see what we were looking at, she quickly looked at the hare and surmised that no

way would she be able to catch it so she just gave me a look and walked toward the camp. As we came around some of the pines that were ringing the camp site the sun stabbed at the air with one last attempt to warm the ground. It stretched out to bathe us in soft golden and orange light. The expanse of the horizon lit from behind lingered just long enough for me to grab my camera and take some of the most vibrant pictures I had yet to take. With the disappearance of the sun we made our way back to the campsite to make dinner and sleep in the quickly advancing night.

The next morning we ate and were off to see if we could make it around the entire peninsula. It was four miles but we had already done more than that on earlier walks. It was cool and I wanted to take some pictures of the canyon. We started out along the uneven ground and found that it was slow going. The vistas that presented themselves before me were spectacular. The ground lay before me unbroken and in pieces. The scattered flora was a silver or grey green. The dogs and I went up and down along the edge of the canyon, looking into the expanse beyond. The light shifted from below the canyon walls with long shadows to bright brilliance and heat. I had to stop many times for the dogs were getting hot fast. We were but half way when I decided to stop and take a short cut back to the camp and take a break. I had taken many pictures before the light climbed too high and I needed to pack up the camp. We cut across the parched land and found the road that cut the peninsula in half. We jogged back along the road with a couple of stops in the shade but we made it back in good time.

I broke camp and we aimed for the head of the peninsula in the jeep. There was a ranger at the end of the peninsula in an overlook and she was explaining the history of the area to a family. I stopped and left the dogs in the car and climbed to the highest point I could find and looked out over the Colorado river and the path it had carved in the earth. How much power and eons of time to sculpt such a spectacle. I took a few pictures but the ones I had taken along the trail were better so I didn't stay long. We packed up and headed out. I was going to see if I could make it up to see another breeder of Entlebuchers's near Salt Lake City, so I needed to get on my way.

CHAPTER 12
MINERAL BOTTOMS
Fear is as strong as you allow it to be.

As we drove out along the mesa, I saw a sign for the mineral bottoms. It said it was an access to the Colorado river. I had taken multiple pictures from the top of the mesa so I said out loud to the dogs. " We should go down there to take pictures and to touch the river. The river I came to see. What do you think guys?" The dogs picked up their heads and just looked at me. As I passed the sign for the turn off, I still hadn't made up my mind. I was still arguing with myself about wasting time or touching the famous river. "Hah, I need to do this, time is not a factor." I said to myself and I turned around at the next turn off and headed back to the pull off for the Mineral Bottoms. I pulled into the turn off and stopped to read the sign that was posted at the entrance. It gave a clear warning that the switch back road was dangerous and could be frightening. Yeah, yeah I thought with my experience in New England of fearful places. I thought I could do it. What the hell.

After about 15 minutes of driving alone on the road I thought I saw dust in the distance. Yup, there was a car pulling a trailer that must have had some kind of boats or rafts on it. It was empty and going pretty fast. I knew that this was a put in for river rafting so I kept going knowing I was getting close. Another twenty minutes had gone by and it still seemed I was no closer to the edge of the mesa. I passed flat topped ridges and the canyon that I was paralleling started to open up wider and wider. The road suddenly opened up and there before me was a parking lot. I stopped and proceeded to look down over the edge. And it wasn't just an edge it was a precipice. I could only see the switch back once. I looked down again and said, "Well if that guy pulling the trailer can do it, then so can I. It can't be that bad." Boy was I wrong. "Could be frightening" wasn't the half of it!!

I got in the jeep and took a long deep breath. I put the jeep in 4 low and headed down. I must have been giving off some serious fearful pheromones because for the first time since we had left our homestead the dogs were hanging their heads over the divider and panting. I had pulled in my mirrors and thank god I did because the track was as wide as the jeep and not much more. The switch backs were definitely that. I crept down the track actually talking to myself. "It's ok, the jeep can handle it. It's ok, the jeep can handle it." Seemed like a good mantra to me. At least I hoped it was. I was starting to sweat with the effort of keeping my focus. I could see that the ground had deep grooves in it to help with traction but I still felt like I needed to talk to "Blue" to give her confidence. It took too long to get down but we did it. I couldn't believe it. I stopped the jeep and looked up. I wiped my sweating hands on my pants, and I started to breathe a little better. "Yahoooo", I exclaimed and the dogs seemed to catch the excitement in my voice. The dogs set back and looked out the windows, seemingly knowing that the danger had passed.

I headed along the track that was at the bottom and we meandered for a while along the river. I found a spot that we could pull into under a cottonwood. I put the jeep in the shadows and we made along the river's edge to a spot where the dogs could wade in. It was muddy and lots of mosquitoes started to buzz me. I took some pictures of the Mesa looming above me and it looked like a long way up. The vertical cliffs that loomed over me took on a different aspect and I felt small. It was wonderful to have this change in perspective, from lofty heights to deep bottom shadows.

We spent some time at the river but the mosquitoes had their way with me and the dogs were not supposed to be out of the car down here, so I made haste and returned to the switch back. I felt that if I didn't return up the trail soon I would not have the power to overcome my fear. If I didn't take the trail up, I would have to drive out and that could take all day and I didn't know if I had enough supplies to do it. I had to look it in the face and say, "No you do not have power over me."

Wasn't that the reason for this trip, to find myself and to look my fears in the eye and take them on. So I headed back to the trailhead and started up. It was slower going because I knew a little more than before, and I was more frightened. The dogs again walked up to the front of the jeep and Bristol started to pant and drool on my shoulder. I didn't pay much attention to it because I could feel my heart racing and my own hands becoming slick on the wheel. I watched as the jeep crawled up the edge of the mesa. I saw then the cars and jeeps that had become before me and had not made it. There were old wrecks and not so old wrecks. "What the hell was I doing?" I asked my self out loud. The dogs swung their heads in my direction but I didn't want to look at them for fear of taking my eyes from the "road". Finally, I could see the cattle grate that marked the top. I crossed it, drove the jeep to the side and started to breath. I took a deep breath and smiled.

"Yes!" I said out loud and Bristol licked my head. I banged on the steering wheel and shouted, "YES! YES!"

I returned to the edge to take pictures but they don't do it justice. The picture in my head that was burned there by adrenaline will never be able to be represented by pictures from a camera. I did it. I did it without anyone else but My Self. The dogs and I returned to the jeep and I knew that I had reached one of the forks in the road of my journey and I had "taken the road less traveled" but that road which once traveled was conquered. I left that mesa with more understanding of myself as a person. I started to find my Self.

What one suspects to be true might not be.

I traveled out of the red and orange desert to the white sands. Then the topography changed again as I entered the mountains of Utah. The green slopes were steep but there were more than the pines I had seen in Colorado. There were broad leaf trees and flowers that I recognized. I sped along the valleys and the fast moving rivers that cut through the mountains looked more familiar than not. It was getting late and I wanted to get to Alpine before it was dark. I had taken a secondary road that cut up through the mountains and it looked like I was almost there on the map. I was going around a bend and there before me were windmills. Lots of windmills.

Wow!

I slowed down a bit and drove under them as the highway opened up to a huge valley. There spread out before me was Salt Lake and the city named after it. The windmills must have been placed at the mouth of the valley to gather the wind that pushed out of the mountains into the great plain before me.

As I left the quiet mountains and silent deserts behind, I immersed myself in traffic and the human race. I sped along the super highway looking for the exit that would take me to the new folks I was to meet tonight.

I made it to the breeder in Alpine Utah about dinnertime and they were great. They opened their house to me and I ate dinner with them and took a shower. We went for a walk and I saw the sun set over Salt Lake City. We talked dogs and she showed me lots of pictures of her dogs and their lineage. It was nice to talk about dogs with someone and be under a roof. I was going to set up the tent but I just told them I would sleep in the car. There were no bugs and I didn't want to set up on their grass. I spent the night listening to the neighborhood put itself to sleep and then I too fell asleep. I woke to pink shafts of light radiating over the mountain peaks. It was ethereal with the star light and the mountains. I crawled to get the camera

and took some pictures. I quietly got into the driver seat and started the day early.

CHAPTER 14
IDAHO
In the immortal words of my amazing sister
"I da ho? no you da ho."

I passed from the white sands of Utah to the flat mesas of Southern Idaho. All of the pictures that I have seen of Idaho were of tall trees and even taller mountains. I came upon the vast open plains of Idaho. It looked nothing like the pictures I had in my mind of this area. I felt no draw to this place. I had the bug to move on outta here. I traveled along the highway in search of a state park to rest that night. The green fields that lay all around me where in funny geometric patterns. Large crane like insects crawled along at a slow speed as they irrigated the land. What would it look like if we had not harnessed the water from below? What would we have done? The sun made a multitude of rainbows as it hit the water sprays from the overly large metal insects. It made it seem just a little more unreal. This was my first encounter with the systems of irrigation. It would not be my last.

I spent the night at one of the original crossings of the Oregon trail. The three islands were spaced out along the Snake River allowing the wagons to go across. It was beautiful. I stood on lush green grass and the sounds of the river were drowned out by the tick tick tick of the sprinklers behind and all around me. The dogs and I walked around the park and felt almost at home. It was so green. If only it was real. Bristol kept

eyeballing the funny sounding water sprays that we passed. I
finally let him take a closer look.

"Go ahead B-, What is it?" with that he walked up to the
sprinkler and bit it. The water sprayed out of his mouth and he
got a great big smile on his face. He looked up at me and it was
like it he was asking me to go at it again. "Ok, but you need to
be e a s y." And I drew out that last word. I could imagine what
he could do to the thing. He took one more look at me and
started to dance with it. It would bounce along spraying the
water and he would keep in time with it as it made a semi circle
around and then back. It was so funny to watch him enjoy
himself. Raven and I watched him for a while and enjoyed
seeing him have fun.

"Ok, Bristol, time to go. Folks might think you will hurt it."
He didn't want to go so I picked up the trailing leash and had to
pull him along. This was Bristol's first encounter with sprinklers
but it would not be his last. Each and every time he would hear
that sound he would get this glint in his eye and just beg me to
let him play with his new friend.

We walked back to the campsite and noticed that we were

alone in our area. They had put sprinklers on either side of us. Suites me I thought, and we ate and then headed to bed. It wasn't long after we ducked into the tent that the wildlife started to come out. We saw a doe and her fawn, a couple of owls and lots of birds. It was like they knew the dogs were not able to get them. It was like the water that sprayed from the ground drew them in, and it probably did. I looked across the river and saw silvery green shrub bushes and not much else. Here on this side where the sprinklers fed the earth it was green. Willows were growing along the river and the grass felt like a carpet under my feet. Oh, the influence of humans, can we ever leave it alone? I thought about this as I took turns watching the fawn graze and the owls hunt in the field behind the tent. I had a lot to think about that night? Could I live here in this area where the impact of humans was so greatly felt. It changed the color, the species, and the use of the land so ultimately. I had to think on that. Did I want to live in a place where the land was so changed by human hands? I had traveled out of the red sands and mesas of Utah into the white sands of Idaho. It was flat and windy here. The hills that rose out of the distance were dotted with sage and scrub. I looked forward to seeing mountains again and to be away from the super highway. I had taken many secondary roads and seen so much more. I longed for the quiet side roads that didn't have constant passing cars and heavy trucks that pushed me aside. I wanted to take to the open roads again. I looked at the map and hoped that I could find a secondary road that would take me across Oregon to the coast.

Needles to broadleaf trees. I found myself immersed in nature and from that immersion ascended a new butterfly fresh and lively. The bonds of the tightly wrapped shell no longer bound her.

I entered Oregon with a sigh of relief. I was now in a place that could hold promise. Maybe I would call this state home. I liked the rolling hills and open fields. It didn't seem so dry here. I was listening to a story about a young boy who was brought up by ghosts. At this point in the story, he was being befriended by some ghouls, and they were in a special place. The scenes that were created by the author were eerily appropriate for what flashed by the car. It was open around me but the road hugged one side of the canyons and therefore I was thrown into shadow more often than not. The black volcanic rock was in contrast to the yellow of the grass that grew up in tufts here and there. Not many folks around here, and not many trees, either. It was lonely out here that was for sure. I spotted a herd of horses in a field next to the road and I noticed that a few of them were mules.

"Hello there, mule. I have one of you guys at home." I told them as I passed. Bristol came up to the barrier and looked at me. "Sorry, buddy, I was talking to the mules out there." And I pointed out to the animals as we sped by. He sat down and just looked out the front windshield. "Ok, ok, I know we have been driving for a while. I will see if we can stop soon near some water so you can swim." I drove on for a while and we came upon some signs for a forest service campground. I wanted to drive through to check it out. I was getting better at this finding a camp thing. So we slowed down and went for a drive around the area. There were some folks here and there, and a deer was in the small field eating grass but the sights were very open so I didn't stop. I did pull of the road farther along the highway and we walked around the area to get some blood back in our legs and we ate a little.

The next forest service campsite I pulled into was occupied too. The locals had moved in and made themselves real comfortable here. I thought it was best to move on since I didn't want to disturb them and I know that Bristol would have had a tough time leaving them alone. I am sure he would have wanted to join them. As I pulled away from the last site, even Raven got up to see the "locals" and as I waved by I yelled out "so long girls" and the locals just tilted their heads and kept

chewing their cud not caring what we did. We drove on for a while and the next site was called Dixie and I had a good feeling about it. Yup, these sites were more wooded and the cattle guard was working so the locals couldn't invade. The dogs and I set up camp and then went to take a long walk.

The walk was great and I took pictures of the forest service road signs so I could follow the pic on the way back. There were a lot of lupines in bloom but the forest was so dense here that I couldn't get great pictures of the landscape. It was nice to be back around trees, but I had to admit I missed the open spaces already. I did hear a wood thrush and thought of home. Lots of wild places here.

I started out early the next day and in minutes of being on the road I started the descent down out of the mountains and into an open prairie area again. It was beautiful. Wooded slopes behind me and in front, wide open spaces that led up to very tall mountains that had almost no vegetation on them. I stopped to take pictures near a real large wagon with red wheels. I was once again on the same land as the first pioneers stood on their trek to Oregon. I was following in their footsteps as one pioneer following another. I, too, was looking for more fertile land and a place to call home. This trip was turning out to have so many parallels. I drove through Prairie City and then up again through the high lands of Redmond and on to the forested peaks of the Sierra Nevada divide. I kept looking around at the sparse open plateau around me and I saw so much human intervention here. It was as if I was back in southern Idaho. The irrigation stretched all along the roadway. I was disappointed to see this and sped along looking forward to reaching the coast. I didn't expect to come around a bend, and there rising up around me were mountains that demanded attention.

Across the flat plateau houses and farms were scattered and behind them like sentries were these mountains. Bright white streaks across black rocks pointing to the sky. The peaks stood out from the lush irrigated fields as if they were erupting out of the ground as if they were floating on fields of green. I had to pull over on a side road to take in what I saw. I sat in the car and tried to figure out how to capture it on film. I took some pictures but I couldn't mimic what lay before me. After some time just looking, I headed into the foothills of the mountains and the peaks were hidden once more.

It was late afternoon now and we had been on the road all day. The dogs were getting restless and I was, too.

I entered Three Sisters and I tried to find a campground but they weren't any sites available. I was still on the eastern side so I decided to head over the divide and try to find a place on the western slopes. I drove past old lava flows and fire scars and on the way down the western slopes, the needles and sparse understory started to be replaced by broadleaf trees and lots of ferns.

   I hit the last one before the national forest ended and hoped that this was the one. I drove around the circle and was overwhelmed by the flora. Green, light green, dark green, drooping tree branches with ferns growing from the cracks in the bark. Yeah, I had found my spot. I unpacked and we headed down below the campsite to the river. This was a camping area for trout fisherman and I could tell. All the sites were backed up to this amazing river that was powerful but meandering at the same time. The light was turning orange and yellow and the trees were actually becoming a deeper green. I had stepped into the world of broadleaf trees once again. The shadows were deepening as the dogs and I waded in the river and we slowly started to unwind. The dogs played in the shallows with logs and sticks and I started to look around for some photo opportunities. It wasn't hard as I was surrounded by lush foliage that hung across the rippling water. It begged to be captured in lights and shadows.

I was in awe of what surrounded me. I had left the silver greens and browns of the eastern forests to immerse myself in a green and yellow world that encircled me in its lattice work of color. I breathed deeply and enjoyed the sounds of the water and birds that I had not heard since I had left Vermont. I criss crossed the river and waded in up to my chest. As I filled up my memory card with the dappled light of the setting sun, I occupied my mind and soul with peace and tranquility of Mother Nature.

We headed back to camp following the sun's rays as it dropped amongst the heavy branches and scattered light across the water. I dried the dogs off as best as I could and we had a cold dinner and got tucked in to bed. We were on the western side of the mountains and the bugs were back. I laid back on my sleeping bag and noticed that once again I looked upon leaves. I had lived amongst needles and sap for weeks now and it was like I was home again. I could hear the wood wren once again and the shadows that fell across the tent were wide and broad not narrow and pointed. I fell asleep to the quiet sounds of the river and the pattern of the dogs breathing. I felt at home here. The next morning we walked along the river once again but the magical light of sunset was gone. It was a cloudy day and the light had difficulty penetrating the thick canopy. We packed up and headed to Veneta. I had contacted more Entle breeders and these folks owned a berry farm. They had said that I could pup the tent in one of their fields and I could meet their dog. I headed out of the mountains passing many small towns that reminded me of Vermont. I was reminded of the contrasting differences though when I would come upon a scarred slope devoid of trees and green. Clear cutting was still allowed here. To see nature raped of what was once a deep forests with so much life was difficult to take. I tried to put miles between those areas and I. I sped down to the coast with new energy to see, touch and smell the ocean. I had traveled so far in miles and within that I had this need to listen to the surf and smell the salt in the air.

CHAPTER 16
BABY STEPS

I had started this journey to find myself, my self. What was self? Was it your soul, your heart, or was it what made you shine from within, what others saw of you? I felt like I had wrestled my body from the cocoon that I had created. Did I bend and shape this protection to keep others out or did I fashion this wall to keep me protected from within? I had faced many fears on this journey and I felt like I was at the beginning of the beginning of my life. I felt a buzzing in my head as I hit I-5 and got closer to the end.

I found Gina's and Kathy's farm and we talked while they were closing up the farm stand. I had mentioned to Gina that the jeep was at the point were I needed an oil change and she jumped on the phone and gave a call to her mechanic.

"Hey, could you take in a friend of mine's jeep for an oil change? It would have to be done today because she is here from Vermont and then heading out early in the morning." I could hear noise on the other end but I couldn't really tell what was being said.

"Sure, I can bring her down right away." Gina hung up and said let's get you over there so we can do this.

"Um, ok." I said. Wow, that was fast I thought. We brought the dogs up to the house and then headed over to her mechanic.

"Thanks so much for fitting me in. I felt the car sort of slip as I was in Colorado and I know I need an oil change." I filled in the mechanic on what I was doing and he was glad to help. He had a jeep of his own and I felt confident that he could do a good job. Gina and I jumped into her car and headed back to the farm so I could eat and take a shower.

It was a nice spot and I felt right at home. I walked around the property with Kathy and talked over a salad that they had collected from their garden. The dogs played outside well together and I felt warm and welcome. I took a welcomed shower and then sat on the veranda and ate dinner with them. Gina and I then went back to get the well oiled and cleaned jeep.
Nice guy ,,Christmas card, talked jeep...

Settled for the night. It felt good to be open to others. I felt confident and secure and this radiated out to those around me. The next morning the dogs and I took a walk up on the hill behind the house and then went for breakfast.   Went to Gina's and Kathy. Enjoyed their space. And farm. Left for the coast... wow loved the coast when it was open and not overrun by large houses one on top of the other. Sun mist, sun mist... wind. Loved it.

CHAPTER 17
OPEN OCEAN OPEN HEART

I walked along the wide expanse laid out before me and I breathed deeply of the salty air. Here I was, finally. My life lay behind me as the new horizon of my future lay before me.

I had traveled across this fine continent finding new parts of my Self and old hidden areas of my heart. I had become comfortable with who I am.

I drove out to the ocean following a river from Venice. It meandered under the bridges that I crossed and finally met its end at the Pacific Ocean. I had started this journey in a land locked state on the other side of the continent and now before me lay the open ocean. I drove along the edge of the dunes and gazed out upon the sand. It seemed as if it went on forever. The low clouds hung over the trees and sand and obstructed my view. It wrapped itself around the jeep as I continued to follow the coast. I longed to get out of the jeep and sit and listen to the surf. It was getting on to lunch and I thought that I would find a spot amongst the coastal towns that I could get lunch at.

I found a seafood place in a quaint little spot and I pulled in. The dogs perked up and I told them to wait. I went in and ordered fish and chips. I went back out to the jeep and gathered the dogs up and we stationed ourselves on the picnic tables over looking the beach and fishing pier.

I ate the best fish and best lunch I had in a long time. I had specialized in salami and cheese for so long I didn't know what real good food was. Yum. I ate it slowly as the sun peeked in and out from the clouds and the gulls and the dogs looked on jealously.

I finished up and shared the fries with them and we then took off north to continue our journey along the coast. I felt drawn to sea the and I needed to feel the sand beneath my toes soon or I would burst. I felt this need to touch the surf and sand with my hand and entire body not just my eyes. There was this pull on me from somewhere out there and I needed to let it take me.

I finally found a spot that had wide open beaches with little sign of human life. I pulled over and the dogs and I pilled out of the jeep. I had this feeling of expectation and I didn't know why. I started down the steep incline towards the sand and the sounds of the surf. The clouds had rolled in so densely that I couldn't see the water. I could hear the murmur of the waves but I couldn't see them. The pull on my body increased.

I watched the dogs play with a stick in the sand and felt joy wash over me as cleanly as the sun. I was right with the world and my Self. I sat on the sand looking out to the sea. I felt as if my life before me was as wide open as the ocean that lapped at my feet. It called to me, whispering that I was ok. In my heart I knew that I would not be the same woman who would be returning to the jeep. I had just climbed down the sand to this spot a moment ago, but it felt as if I had spent a hundred years getting here. I no longer felt the fatigue of uncertainty, the confusion of what I was to do with my life. I had finally let go of the last layer of fear.

I felt compelled to lift my face to the sun, wind, and water that surrounded me. I felt whole. I felt complete. I felt unbroken for the first time.

EPILOGUE
HOME

I took the exit off the highway and it seemed like I had been gone for longer than 7 weeks. I took the habitual turn onto my road and looked around with new eyes. I missed this place. It was so bright and sunny. It was as if I had taken the Sunlight with me from my trip and brought it along. I stopped at the bridge over the brook and took a quick picture of Tiny's house and we took the right on to Snipe Island. We slowly drove up to Canine Run and I stopped and took a picture of the road sign. It had a vine growing up it and the sign was partially covered by a small tree that was not there when I left. I turned down the driveway and headed to Tiny's house.

I pulled up to the house and she was coming out with a camera and Mylo. A smile was plastered across her face as she walked down the steps. I got out and let the dogs jump out.
"Go see Aunty." I told the kids.
"Welcome back," she said.
"Thanks, it feels good to be home." I replied. "It's so green and everything has grown so much."
"Yeah, it hasn't stopped raining all summer. I am so tired of the rain."
"Guess I brought the sun with me." I smiled as I said these such

true words.

"Hmm let's see how long it lasts." She grimaced.

"OK I need to get home I will come down later."

I shouted for the dogs and they came a running. "Load up" and they jumped in. I think they wanted to see home as much as I did. I turned the car around and took out the camera. I started the video as we slowly crawled up the driveway. It had been eroded since the last time we had driven it. I wondered if Herbert was around. I later found out that he had been busy all summer and now there were 4 more little Herberts.

I stopped at the fields and slowly swung the camera back and forth to take it in. They were so vacant, not goats, no mule or horse. It was like they were standing there waiting for something. It didn't feel right to be so alone here on the driveway with only the dogs.

I started up the rest of the way to the house. I pulled in to my spot and took a picture of the mileage that the dogs and I had covered together. Six thousand, one hundred and twenty four point seven miles. Wow. It couldn't do the amount of mileage I had covered in my soul justice. I had come from so far beyond, that it would have not equaled it even if I had taken a trip to Saturn and back. I had come so much farther than miles.

The dogs got out of the car and we walked up to the house. I was back. But was I home? I had found so much of myself in the wide open spaces of the west. The tall trees that lifted to the sky, the pounding surf that pulled me out to sea. Was that where I belonged?

Since this trip I have run two half marathons, taken a six month trip back across the continent and made many new discoveries about what determination can allow you to do. I look forward to continuing to look out and to see new opportunities before me. Enjoy.

I want to thank all the friends who helped me write this book. I want to especially thank Angie and Tiny for being part of this project and for being editors. Many thanks go to Jerry for doing the final edit. For Joyce goes the grand prize, for getting me started in this endeavor!

Made in the USA
Lexington, KY
14 July 2011